P9-AOT-771

Planning and Politics in the Metropolis

Metropolitan America:
Its Government and Politics Series

Under the Editorship of
Alan K. Campbell
Dean of the Maxwell Graduate School
of Citizenship and Public Affairs

Planning and Politics in the Metropolis

David C. Ranney
Assistant Professor
Department of Regional Planning
University of Wisconsin

Charles E. Merrill Publishing Company
Columbus, Ohio
A Bell & Howell Company

Standard Book Number 675-09531-9
Library of Congress Catalog Card Number: 69-14520

7 8 9 10—80, 79,

Printed in the United States of America

To Omar S. Ranney

Preface

Planning has become a growing concern of governments in metropolitan areas. The purpose of this book is to provide the reader with a better understanding of the planning function. Emphasis will be placed on an understanding of how public planning policy is developed by the governments in metropolitan areas. Some specific questions to be explored will be: what is the planner's role in local government; what kinds of factors influence the planner as he makes planning decisions; how are these decisions transformed into planning policy through the local governments? In keeping with the purpose of the series, of which this text is a part, primary emphasis will be placed on the key role which the phenomenon of metropolitanism plays in the development of planning policy.

A number of individuals have contributed suggestions and other types of assistance which I would like to acknowledge. Alan K. Campbell, the editor of the series originally suggested that I undertake the writing of this book. His suggestions and encouragement proved to be invaluable. My colleague Philip Meranto read the entire text and made many useful comments from the perspective of a political scientist and a student of metropolitan affairs. A number of other individuals read various portions of the manuscript and contributed a significant number of ideas which appear in the book. These include Peter Amato, Leo Jakobson, and Robert Mendelson. My research assistant, Philip Mummert, provided a variety of forms of assistance including substantive criticism and information gathering. My mother, Dee M. Ranney, donated her considerable talents as a professional writer by making editorial comments on the entire manuscript. My wife, Roberta Ranney, contributed editorial and substantive comments and generally helped put the manuscript together. To all of these people I am very grateful.

David C. Ranney
Madison, Wisconsin

Contents

List of Tables

List of Figures

Planning in the Metropolis: An Overview 1

The present chapter provides an overview of the subject matter to be covered in this book. We begin by developing an operational definition of planning. With this definition as a base, a number of theoretical views of what planning ought to entail are introduced. Theory is then compared with what most planners are actually doing. Finally, a theoretical model of planning policy formulation is introduced as a basis for the organization of the rest of the book.

What Is Planning?

One difficulty inherent in any discourse on planning is that of defining the scope of the discussion. Unlike most other governmental activities such as police, fire, public works, and education, the planning function lacks a clearly defined scope of activity. Within any given government, planning duties may be well defined, but the definition varies considerably from government to government. The definition adhered to in a particular community is very important. To a great extent it determines the governmental and political issues that are generated by the planning function.

One generalization that can be made about the planning function of local government is that it tends to focus its attention on the use of physical space. This does not mean that all of the planning done by local governments has such a focus. Many kinds of governmental activities are planned. But the local governmental function called "planning" is primarily concerned with the use of physical space.

In order to understand the distinction between public planning and planning as a function of local government, it is necessary to briefly examine the nature of planning in its broadest sense. One very broad definition suggests that planning is

> . . . clarifying one's objectives and then determining what action shall be taken by whom, when, by what methods, and at what costs in order to achieve the desired goals.[1]

Within this broad definition, planning can be either functionally or project oriented.[2] Planning is functional when it develops an appropriate course of action for decision makers within a particular field. The site planner on an urban renewal project, for example, is concerned with arranging the proposed buildings harmoniously. He is planning the arrangement of buildings and space on the basis of such considerations as functional adequacy, proper communication and circulation, reasonable cost, promotion of health and comfort, and aesthetic features.[3] Project oriented planning is broader than functional planning. It involves a reconciliation of numerous and diversified functional considerations. To use the urban renewal example again, the project oriented planner would plan the courses of action to be taken by a variety of decision makers. Planning all of the procedures for an urban renewal project would be based on a broad set of objectives. Aside from the physical criteria, the project planner must deal with engineering, sociological, economic, and political objectives. Thus project planning is highly complex and requires a tremendous interdisciplinary effort.

Functional and project oriented planning may be applied to practically every human endeavor. Professional planners are currently being hired by business and industry, the military and the governments. Within the governments, planning is being done by many different

---

[1]Marshall Edward Dimock, and Gladys Ogden Dimock, *Public Administration* (3rd ed.; New York: Holt, Rinehart and Winston, Inc., 1964), p. 131.

[2]Melville C. Branch, *Planning: Aspects and Applications* (New York: John Wiley & Sons, Inc., 1966), pp. 10-11.

[3]Kevin Lynch, *Site Planning* (Cambridge: The M.I.T. Press, 1962), pp. 11-14.

administrative agencies. Governmental executives from the President, governors, and mayors, to city managers are employing planners for a wide range of public activities. Thus to keep our discussion manageable, it is necessary to focus our attention on public planning which emphasizes the use of physical space.

One might well ask what is the purpose of planning the use of physical space? An observer has suggested that a "... progression toward higher levels of material, aesthetic, social, and even spiritual satisfaction for the urban citizen ..."[4] is a major concern of such physical planning. Others have suggested that there are social and economic costs resulting from non-planning. Slums, congestion, noise, dirt, air and water pollution, overcrowded and inadequate schools, unemployment, inadequate municipal services, disease, crime, ugliness and a wide variety of other ills[5] are the results of non-planning. Planning attempts to minimize such costs. In short, physical planning aims to control the physical development of communities, thus avoiding the major social and economic costs of non-planning. Hopefully the result will be a progressively better environment for urban dwellers.

Although planners tend to think of environment in physical terms, appropriate standards for the use of physical space must consider the political, economic and social goals of the community. "Physical" questions concerning such things as the intensity of land use, the stock of housing in various price ranges, the need for and location of various types of community facilities, the appropriate relationship between land uses, and transportation patterns are rooted in the social and economic values of the community. Thus, the issues of physical planning are not entirely physical and therefore are not always subject to strictly technical solutions.

Furthermore, physical planning bears a distinct relationship to many other governmental functions. Decisions about the patterns and location of transportation lines will involve not only the local planning agency but federal, state and local highway departments, public works departments and city engineers. The location of highways will have an impact on the location of other land uses and will affect the land use policies of communities throughout a given metropolis. Res-

---

[4]Lowdon Wingo, Jr., ed., *Cities and Space: The Future Use of Urban Land* (Baltimore: The Johns Hopkins Press, 1963), p. 3.

[5]See for example Catherine Bauer Wurster, "Framework for an Urban Society," in President's Commission on National Goals, *Goals for Americans* (New York: Prentice-Hall, Inc., Spectrum Books, 1960), pp. 225-248.

idential density patterns and the location of housing within various price ranges will have an impact on education, the need for public works and police and fire services. Decisions about the proper location of industry can have a major impact on employment and income levels. The level of income determines the ability of people to purchase the things which they feel they need for a comfortable life. Income also determines the ability of people to pay for the public services which they require. All of these interrelationships imply a need for some coordination of activities to accompany physical planning.

Thus, although the present volume will focus most of its attention on planning the use of physical space, there will still be a broad range of subject matter to cover. Because the range of potential subject matter in the field of physical planning is so great, planning theoreticians have expressed a variety of viewpoints concerning what the planning function is and what those working within the framework of that function ought to be doing.

Planning and Theory

At the turn of the century the first American planners placed a great emphasis on the physical criteria for determining how to use urban space. Standards for the location and space requirements of different land uses such as housing, recreation, industry, etc., tended to be very rigid and were based on certain "design concepts." For example, the belief that different land uses should be kept separate and that densities should be low were accepted as land use standards. Many of the first members of the planning profession were persons of engineering and/or architectural backgrounds who tended to reinforce the profession's physical bias. Plan making did involve socio-economic research such as population and economic studies. But until quite recently, the planning profession paid very little attention to how these studies were to be used in formulating land use standards. The "design solution" to our urban ills was the predominant method of planning. Such "solutions" were the result of a creative and artistic process whereby physical "design concepts" were adapted to meet specific situations. The "solutions" were rarely based upon rigorous social science research. Underlying this physical emphasis in early planning practice was the view that physical environment was at the root of urban problems. Thus it was presumed that an improvement in the physical environment would lead to an improvement in all the social and economic problems besetting urban communities.

While much of planning practice still reflects a physical bias, many planners are beginning to take a broader view. More attention is being given to the manner in which social science research can contribute to formulating plans for the use of urban land. The most recent edition of a widely used textbook by F. Stuart Chapin illustrates this point.[6] Chapin expresses the view that there are a number of determinants of land use patterns. Among these determinants, Chapin cites social processes and behavior; economic variables such as property value, employment opportunity, fiscal productivity and transportation costs; physical characteristics of the land; and the nature of local political systems. Chapin stresses the importance of forming planning goals based on local values. Once goals are established, Chapin suggests the planner should make a detailed set of social, economic and physical studies. The studies are then used to develop location and space standards for different land uses. The standards provide a basis for a plan that reflects community goals.

The link between social science research and the development of physical plans has been strengthened by a number of recent research efforts. Economists and regional scientists have been exploring the relationships between the location of land uses and numerous socioeconomic variables. This exploration has produced new knowledge about the relationship between the location of economic activity and economic health. Ideas about the determinants of land use location have also come out of these efforts.[7] A closely related line of inquiry has resulted in the development of mathematical models that simulate urban development. Models simulating the impact of alternative urban transportation plans on land use have been used in a few metropolitan areas.

These developments relating social science research to location and space standards in land use planning have broadened the early emphasis on physical design concepts. Along with these advancements in

---

[6]F. Stuart Chapin, Jr., *Urban Land Use Planning* (2nd ed.; Urbana: University of Illinois Press, 1965).

[7]The application of traditional economic concepts to the economy of urban areas has begun to interest many economists. See, for example, Wilbur R. Thompson, *A Preface to Urban Economics* (Baltimore: The Johns Hopkins Press, 1965). Much of regional science involves application of input-output analysis to problems of the location of economic activity. Examples may be found in *The Proceedings of the Regional Science Association* and the *Journal of Regional Science* as well as the works of Walter Isard, *Location and Space Economy* (New York and Cambridge: John Wiley & Sons, Inc. and Technology Press, 1956). For examples of research in the determinants of land use location see F. Stuart Chapin, Jr. and Shirley F. Weiss, *Urban Growth Dynamics* (New York: John Wiley & Sons, Inc., 1962); also see some of the literature on mathematical models and land use. Some of these models are explained in a special issue of *Journal of the American Institute of Planners*, Vol. XXXI, No. 2, (May, 1965).

the research area, theoretical formulations of the planning process have begun to emphasize the complexity of urban developmental relationships. The simulation model building referred to above has contributed to a better understanding of this complexity. Other theoretical formulations have viewed the development of urban areas as a spatial adaptation to the search of interdependent urban activities for a location that minimizes communication costs.[8] Some theoreticians have used the technique of gaming simulation to learn more about the complexities of urban development. This technique asks individuals to assume the roles of different actors in the planning process and to make decisions in accord with their roles in a simulated decision making environment. These individuals then see the impact of their decisions on a hypothetical community. This technique has been used largely as an educational device dramatically illustrating how a variety of variables influence the development of urban areas.[9]

The recent emphasis on the complexities of the development of urban communities has led to considerable soul searching on the part of many members of the planning profession. The traditional emphasis on the use of physical space has been questioned. Some of this thinking has led to pleas that certain neglected aspects of planning analysis be singled out and considered. Some planners, for example, have expressed concern over the neglect of the social consequences of planning activities. They have suggested that specific measures be undertaken to produce "social plans."[10] Also singled out for special attention has been the determination of the political implications of planning action.[11]

---

[8]Richard L. Meier, *Communications Theory of Urban Growth* (Cambridge: The M.I.T. Press, 1962).

[9]Richard L. Meier, "Gaming Simulation in Urban Planning," *Planning* (1965), pp. 286-293; Richard D. Duke, "Gaming Urban Systems," *Planning* (1965), pp. 293-300; Richard L. Meier and Richard D. Duke, "Gaming Simulation for Urban Planning," *Journal of the American Institute of Planners* (January, 1966), pp. 3-16; Alan G. Feldt, "Operational Gaming in Planning Education," *Journal of the American Institute of Planners* (January, 1966), pp. 17-22.

[10]Harvey Perloff, "New Directions in Social Planning," *Journal of the American Institute of Planners* (November, 1965), pp. 297-303. For a discussion of the meaning of social planning see: John W. Dyckman, "Social Planning, Social Planners and Planned Societies," *Journal of the American Institute of Planners* (March, 1966), pp. 66-75.

[11]See Alan Altshuler, *The City Planning Process: A Political Analysis* (Ithaca: Cornell University Press, 1966); for an interesting and thoughtful effort to develop a framework for analyzing the political implications of planning decisions, see Sheldon J. Lustig, "Political Base Analysis: A Framework for Developing Planning Strategy and Implementing Actions," (Unpublished Master's thesis, Syracuse University, June, 1966).

Most of the recent thinking about the proper scope of the planning function has moved away from the idea of compartmentalizing planning into physical, economic and social components. Instead, a number of planning theorists are attempting to devise a systematic approach that will allow different kinds of planning to be welded together. The view that the planner's role is to devise meaningful alternative plans and then develop a systematic basis for choosing among these alternatives illustrates this kind of thinking. Davidoff and Reiner have advocated a "choice theory of planning" which suggests that the planning process should involve a series of choices. Choices must be made among alternative goals and means of achieving these goals.[12] The authors suggest the need to develop broad criteria for making these choices. In a separate article, Davidoff suggests that in a given community there should be several different plans representing diverse values. Davidoff conceives of these plans as statements of policy covering a broad range of subject matter. He proposes that different planners act as advocates of the values of diverse groups in a community.[13] Both articles imply that planning activity in government must contend with the economic, social, and physical values that exist in the community. Reiner and Davidoff suggest that planning as a function of local government should be concerned with the development of all governmental policies relevant to deciding future courses of action.

Henry Fagin is another proponent of a planning function which would deal with a broad range of subject matter.[14] He conceives of planning as an action-oriented activity involving research, goal formation, plan making, coordination, general assistance and advice. Fagin argues that these planning activities have been diffused among a variety of agencies within government. He proposes that the responsibility for preparing the physical plan, the budget or financial plan, and the general programming of governmental activity be combined within one governmental agency which would undertake the creation of a broad "policies plan." The "policies plan" concept would have the effect of bringing all of the planning activities of government into a single planning agency.

---

[12]Paul Davidoff and Thomas A. Reiner, "A Choice Theory of Planning," *Journal of the American Institute of Planners* (May, 1962), pp. 103-115.

[13]Paul Davidoff, "Advocacy and Pluralism in Planning," *Journal of the American Institute of Planners* (November, 1965), pp. 331-338.

[14]Henry Fagin, "Organizing and Carrying Out Planning Activities Within Urban Government," *Journal of the American Institute of Planners* (August, 1957), pp. 109-114.

A concept of "policy planning" similar to Fagin's has been expressed in the Federal Government's recent Model Cities Legislation. The program guide to the Demonstration Cities and Metropolitan Development Act of 1966 states that this act

> . . . calls for a comprehensive attack on social, economic and physical problems in selected slum and blighted areas through the most effective and economical concentration and coordination of Federal, State, and local public and private efforts.[15]

The guidelines for the application for funds under this act stress the need to establish an agency to coordinate all of the social, economic and physical development activities in the community. To achieve this, the guidelines suggest the model cities agency utilize innovative techniques to establish priorities among programs and to evaluate the progress of programs once they are under way. New applications of systems analysis, program budgeting and cost-benefit analysis are emphasized as appropriate methods for establishing priorities and coordinating program implementation.

It is clear that many planning theorists and some recent programs of the Federal Government have moved away from the physical emphasis of planning. It must be stressed, however, that these theoretical notions and planning practice are two different matters. As noted at the beginning of this chapter, planning as a function of local government is presently concerned with the use of physical space. The physical planning activities of government may be based upon broad social science research or upon narrower design considerations. In either case the focus of planning is on land use.

The Planner's Work

In order to understand how decisions on the future use of space are made in local government, it is necessary to generalize on the array of activities, techniques, and tools that define the nature of the planner's work. What does the planner do in his office each day?

In practice the planner engages in two basic kinds of activities. He develops plans, and he assists in the implementation of these plans.

---

[15]U. S. Department of Housing and Urban Development, *Improving the Quality of Urban Life: A Program to Model Neighborhoods in Demonstrations Cities* (Washington: U. S. Government Printing Office, December, 1966), p. 1.

Planners are often called upon to administer a variety of legal tools and to participate in certain programs and advisory activities. These tools, programs, and advice are primarily concerned with plan implementation. The major legal tools are zoning, subdivision regulations, and building codes. The programs are those funded by the Federal Government such as urban renewal, community renewal, and other national programs. In addition, the planner is called upon to make recommendations on sites for highways, hospitals, schools and other community facilities. In some cities the planner is responsible for scheduling capital expenditures to be made by the government.

The development of land use plans is considered the central activity of planning by many professionals. Plan making should be an ongoing process. Once an initial planning document is developed, it ought to be constantly under review by the planning agency in order to keep it in line with the current developmental trends. Methods of plan making vary considerably from agency to agency.[16] The planning process should begin with a general evaluation of local conditions and problems. This evaluation and the views of public and private groups and individuals form a basis for the development of a set of planning goals. Next, detailed technical studies are made. Some of these deal with characteristics of the land. Analysis of the physical features of the land, the existing land use, the structural and aesthetic quality of individual structures, valuation patterns of land and improvements, as well as public attitudes about land use are examples of urban land studies. Economic research should also be an important part of the initial set of technical studies. Such studies evaluate existing and projected employment opportunity and general economic conditions. Economic base, input-output analysis, and employment forecasting can be used to evaluate and understand the local economy. A third area is fiscal research. The costs of local public services and the public revenues generated by land use patterns should be one of the initial planning studies. Studies of the social structure of the communi-

---

[16]The text by F. Stuart Chapin contains a detailed analysis of the elements of land use planning. Chapin views the planning process as a series of successive policy decisions based on substantial socio-economic research and presented in the form of a planning document that is constantly under revision. Chapin, *op. cit.* In practice plans are usually not the progressive and dynamic documents that Chapin pictures, but in his description the details of forming a plan are included. He does not deal with the smaller scale design problems involved in site planning such as a shopping center or a central business district. Such a discussion may be found in Kevin Lynch, *op. cit.* The present discussion of land use planning is based on Chapin.

ty are also important. Social research provides information about the activities of those who use urban facilities, their attitudes on various planning issues, and the location of persons with varying socio-economic and attitudinal characteristics. Finally, population forecasts must be made to determine how many people will be living in the community at various future times.

Once these studies have been made, they can become the basis for the rest of the plan. A determination of the need for particular land uses such as streets, housing in various price ranges, shopping facilities, manufacturing and wholesaling establishments, recreation etc., can be made. In addition, location standards are devised for these uses based partly on the technical studies and partly on factors such as need for accessibility, convenience, compatibility with surrounding uses, and security.[17] Space requirements for land users are established after the future demand for each use is determined. Demand estimates are based on socio-economic trends and the goals established earlier. The location and space requirements are brought together during the final phase of plan making. The end product is a recommendation for the future use of the land.[18]

Once the plan is completed, it is adopted by the planning agency. The agency usually presents the plan to the governing body and attempts to have the plan adopted. If the plan becomes an official document, it must then be implemented either through redevelopment or through future actions of the government that affect the use of land.[19] The zoning ordinance[20] is one implementative tool which almost all local planning agencies utilize. In theory the zoning ordinance ought to be the legislative expression of the land use plan, however, in practice, zoning ordinances are occasionally developed by the planners without a plan. In either case, zoning ordinances do exist in most cities. A zoning ordinance is a municipal law which divides a municipality into districts. Within these districts, standards and restrictions are established for the use of land. The restrictions may involve: the type of land use (residential, commerical, industrial,

---

[17]Chapin, *op. cit.*, pp. 370-382.

[18]This discussion of plan making has been highly oversimplified. Students wishing to go into more detail on planning techniques should consult the sources cited at the beginning of this discussion.

[19]It should be stressed that the development, revision and implementation of the plan are all critical parts of a continuous process. In the present discussion the parts are separated for purposes of conceptual clarity.

[20]A good explanation of zoning may be found in: William I. Goodman and Eric C. Freund, eds., *Principles and Practice of Urban Planning* (4th ed.; Washington: International City Managers' Association, 1968), Chapter 15.

etc.); the height and bulk of structures; the size of front, back and side yards; and the size of lots.

The legal basis of zoning is very complex. Consequently, the administration of the zoning ordinance takes up a great deal of a planner's time. Zoning is a restriction on the use of private property which is imposed by the government. In order to be constitutional the ordinance must promote the public health, safety, morals, or general welfare. If the ordinance can satisfy this requirement then the municipality can constitutionally enforce it as a part of municipal police power.[21] Aside from constitutional requirements, most municipal zoning ordinances must satisfy state statutes regulating zoning. Their zoning authority is derived from the state legislature. In later chapters we will discuss differences in state statutes which apply to local zoning. The necessity for many municipalities to show that their zoning ordinance meets the requirements of state statutes adds to the complexity of the legal aspects of zoning.

The difficulties of applying zoning law to the administration of the zoning ordinance are largely derived from the fact that most zoning ordinances were preceded by the development of the municipalities. Those properties which violate the zoning ordinance but which existed prior to the adoption of the ordinance are called "non-conforming uses." Properties designated as non-conforming uses are not allowed to expand or to be significantly improved. Difficulties emerge when the owner of such property wants to improve it or when the owner of a given piece of property discovers that it will be to his advantage to improve that property in a manner that is not consistent with the zoning ordinance. In such cases an individual property owner can either challenge the legality of the zoning ordinance, seek an amendment to the ordinance, or ask that an exception or variance be granted for his property. In all cases the planner must spend a great deal of time reviewing the claims of those who want the zoning ordinance changed, determining how the proposed changes relate to the plan, and making recommendations to the governing body.

Zoning is only one of planning's implementative tools; another is the subdivision regulation. Subdivision regulations are municipal laws that control the development of new residential areas. The width and pattern of streets, the facilities for drainage and lighting, the size and shape of lots, the provisions for open space, sewer and water systems,

---

[21]The constitutionality of the zoning ordinance was established in the Supreme Court case of *Village of Euclid v. Ambler Realty Company*, 272 (U.S.), 36 (1926).

and the grading, surfacing and curbing of streets are examples. Planners are generally given the responsibility for preparing subdivision regulations and for reviewing proposed subdivision plans once an ordinance has been passed.

The building code is a third kind of implementative device. The enforcement of codes which provide for minimum standards for the structure and facilities of buildings are a part of the municipal police power. For this reason they must be designed to protect the health, safety, morals and general welfare of the public. Planners are sometimes involved in both the writing and enforcement of these codes.

Another implementative device is renewal. The program which is partially financed by the Federal Government and known as "urban renewal" is the most common device. Under this program the Federal Government underwrites from two-thirds to three-fourths of the cost of urban renewal projects. These projects involve conservation of the quality of developed properties, the rehabilitation of developments that are in poor condition, and the redevelopment of property when structures are beyond repair. Urban renewal is usually administered separately from planning, however, but planners are involved in the administration of the program, in the designation of sites that are to be redeveloped, and in the preparation of the overall urban renewal plan.

One further means of implementing plans is the capital improvement program. Capital programming is a form of financial planning. In preparing a capital improvement program the planner goes to each department of the municipality and determines the nature and cost of all proposed projects which cannot be financed out of current revenues. He then establishes priorities for these projects, determines how they can be financed and schedules their implementation. In essence the capital program is a means of coordinating governmental investments.

These five implementative devices and the development of plans comprise the day-to-day work of the planner. The emphasis placed on these various activities in particular planning offices will vary considerably. In some places there is no plan making function as such. The planner may spend all of his time doing studies and administering the zoning ordinance. In other places planning may involve all of these activities. The emphasis on planning activities in a specific situation may depend on the training of the planners involved. It may also depend on the kinds of instructions and budget the planner receives from governmental officials.

Planning as a Governmental Function

Planning, which includes some or all of the activities discussed above, may be administered by municipal, county, multi-county, or other regional agencies. Although planning originated in municipalities, the development of metropolitan areas containing many cities and municipalities has led to the establishment of planning agencies that plan for regions which include many municipalities.

The fact remains that most local planning is done by the individual municipal governments within the metropolitan areas. Although more area-wide planning efforts are taking place, such efforts have not had much impact. In a 1964 study of metropolitan planning activities it was concluded that metropolitan planning agencies have neither the funds nor the legal authority to "perform functions keyed to managing regional development."[22]

Planning as Public Policy

Banfield and Wilson have observed that governments perform two kinds of functions.[23] One function involves the supply of public goods and services. Within municipal planning, the planner fulfills this service by devising a plan, selecting sites for public facilities, administering the zoning ordinance and building codes, and a host of other activities. Municipal governments perform many other service functions. Garbage is collected, police and fire protection provided, and streets maintained. At the same time governments are serving another kind of function which Banfield and Wilson call conflict management. Conflict management, the subject matter of politics, involves the resolution of disputes over the performance or lack of performance of governments' service function (including planning).

Practically everything government does can bring about a conflict of some sort. The hiring of public personnel can lead to disputes between the government and various groups who feel they are not getting a fair share of the jobs available. Conflict may arise over the

---

[22]The Joint Center for Urban Studies of the Massachusetts Institute of Technology and Harvard University, *The Effectiveness of Metropolitan Planning*, prepared in cooperation with the Subcommittee on Intergovernmental Relations of the Committee on Government Operations, United States Senate (Washington: U. S. Government Printing Office, June 30, 1964).

[23]Edward C. Banfield and James Q. Wilson, *City Politics* (Cambridge, Mass.: Harvard University Press and the M.I.T. Press, 1963), pp. 18-22.

amount of taxes needed to finance governmental services. The administration of particular functions can become a point of conflict. Questions such as which streets should be repaved next year, the number of garbage collections per week, or the location of a hospital or library can lead to disagreements among various segments of a community. Somehow these conflicts must be resolved. Otherwise continual dissatisfaction could erupt into violence. In the American governmental system the management or resolution of conflict is the responsibility of elected officials. It is their job to satisfy the electorate. The penalty for failure is rejection at election time. Thus, conflict management is just as important to the efficient operation of government as the professional provision of services.

As Banfield and Wilson point out, these two functions of government are performed simultaneously. In some instances the service function is dominant or more evident, while in other situations public policy is formed largely through conflict management. Not only do these statements about the relationship between the service and conflict management functions apply to government generally, they also have specific applicability to the planning function. In practice, planners tend to base their decisions on professional standards and ideologies which are acquired through training and experience. At the same time, however, the criteria for planning the use of urban space are not totally objective, but are based on a series of value premises. Some of these premises underlie the professional standards on which planning decisions are based. Other values tend to determine the manner in which such standards are applied.[24] If the planner must base his decisions on values, it follows that a planning decision is not simply right or wrong. Planners using differing value premises may arrive at entirely different decisions concerning the "correct" planning policy. Since planning decisions are complicated by values, there is a potential for conflict over the provision of the planning services. Some of this conflict is managed by the planner himself through compromise with his adversaries or through adjustments in his decisions to correspond with political reality. Other conflicts arising over planning decisions may be resolved by the elected decision makers who are ultimately responsible for the final form of all public policy.

The mechanisms through which municipal planning policy is formed are thus a product of the performance of professional planning

---

[24]Some of the value premises of planning will be discussed in later chapters. For another source which supports the view taken here see: Paul Davidoff, "Advocacy and Pluralism in Planning," *op. cit.*, pp. 331-338.

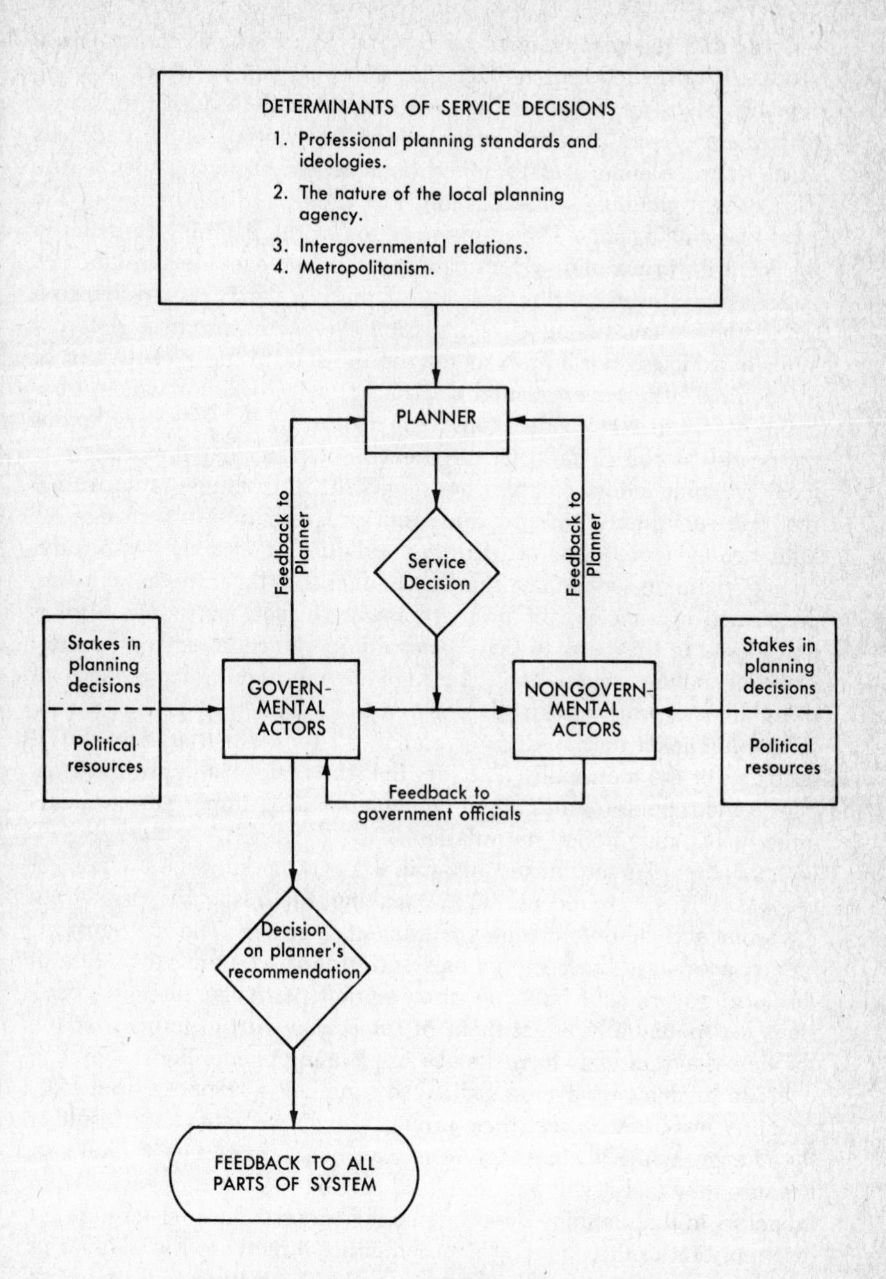

Figure 1

A Model of Planning Decision Making

services and the management of conflict. An overview of the entire process is presented on page 15. This flow diagram indicates that the planner makes an initial set of decisions labeled "service," including plan making and plan implementation. The initial set of decisions made by the planner is determined by a variety of factors such as the professional planning standards and ideologies, and the nature of the local planning agency. The formal location of the planning function in the local governmental system can have an influence on the kinds of decisions produced by this function. If the planner is responsible to a semi-independent planning commission, he might produce different kinds of policies than if he is merely on the staff of the executive or of the council. Intergovernmental relations is a third factor which influences planning service decisions. The nature of the urban programs sponsored by the Federal Government is of particular importance to local planning efforts. Public housing, "701" planning grants, urban renewal, community renewal, and other programs have a considerable influence over the kinds of planning activities undertaken. Also influencing planning service decisions is the fact that this function is being performed in a metropolitan environment. In fact, metropolitanism is considered in this book to be of central importance in explaining local planning policy formulation. The high degree of interdependence of the many govermental jurisdictions within the metropolis has a considerable impact on the kinds of planning issues which arise in different parts of the metropolis. The fact that the plans of the governments within metropolitan areas affect one another is an important consideration of planning policy formulation.

Once the planner makes his initial decision known, a chain of responses is apt to occur. Those making the responses are either governmental actors or non-governmental actors. The non-governmental actors are those individuals and groups who are not a part of the local government but who discover that particular planning decisions can potentially affect them in some way. In the terms used on the flow diagram, they have a stake in planning policy. For example, a decision to change a zoning ordinance can elicit a response from local property owners who feel their property will lose value as a result of the change, while business interests may be in support of the change because they feel it will help the local economy. Such non-governmental actors in the planning decision making process will register support or opposition to the planning decision either directly to the planner or to other governmental officials or to both. The nature and extent of involvement of non-governmental actors in a planning decision will depend on the stakes they have in a particular decision as well as on their political resources or their ability to influence public officials.

Reaction to initial planning decisions may also come directly from the mayor or manager, the council, or from other governmental actors. Again, the nature of this reaction will depend on the stakes of individual governmental actors and the political resources at their disposal. Stakes in planning decisions may develop through pressure (feedback) from the non-governmental actors. Pressure put upon the executive or members of council by influential community leaders regarding a particular planning decision may cause these officials to take an interest in planning which they would not have had otherwise. Governmental actors, excluding the planner, make their views on planning decisions felt in two ways: by making their views known to the planner (feedback); or by taking formal action or inaction on the planner's recommendations.

When diverse reactions to the planner's service decisions occur, there is conflict. The existence of such conflict gives rise to the need for conflict management. Part of the conflict management function may be assumed by the planner himself if he revises his initial decision on the basis of the feedback he has received (or thinks he might receive). The remainder of the conflict management function is performed by the chief executive and/or members of council. These officials have the ultimate authority to act or not to act on the planner's recommendations. Once the chief executive and/or the council decide what to do about the planner's recommendation, the effects of that decision feed back to all parts of the system and have an impact on the future actions of all actors in the planning process.

This brief explanation of the model of planning decision making will be elaborated in the pages to follow. The model is, in fact, the basis for the organization of this volume. The next four chapters deal with the determinants of the planner's service decisions. Chapter 2 traces the development of certain professional planning attitudes and standards. Some of the ideologies which underlie these attitudes and standards are also discussed. Chapters 3 and 4 deal with the governmental context of planning, stressing the impact of local planning institutions and intergovernmental relations on the performance of the planning function. Chapter 5 discusses the key role of metropolitanism in local planning decision making. In Chapter 6, the nature of conflict and conflict management in the performance of the planning function is explored. Chapter 7 presents some hypotheses about the reasons behind political involvement in local planning issues. A final chapter summarizes the entire discussion.

2 Physical Design, Utopias, and Reform: The Planners' Heritage

The nature of the recommendations made by planners in any given city will be partially a reflection of their attitudes. Among the attitudes which might have the most influence on the planner's recommendations are those relating to his professional standards of city planning and his attitude toward his local government. Since professional attitudes are partially formed by training and experience, individual planners will vary considerably in their beliefs. Further, the state of planning "theory" is so unclear at the present time that there is no consistent and generally agreed upon set of professional views. However, the planning profession does possess a certain heritage which exerts considerable influence over the formal training of many planners. This heritage has an impact on the way in which planners interpret the experiences they have in the field, and it is an important part of the process by which planning decisions are made.

The purpose of the present chapter is to examine the evolution of the planning function in the United States and elsewhere in order to understand how the planners' heritage can influence planning decisions. A basic assumption of this chapter is that a series of historical developments have produced three types of attitudes which strongly influence present planning policy formulation. These attitudes are:

1. that the physical environment is a major determinant of the "good" community;
2. that an "ideal" physical design for communities can be utilized as a basis for physical land use standards;
3. that "politicians" cannot be trusted.

Physical Design and the "Good" Community

The fact that the practice of urban planning tends to focus its attention on physical land use rather than on broader socio-economic concerns is in part a reflection of the planners' heritage. Planners have been accused of believing that all of the city's ills can be cured by adjustments in the physical environment. The idea that many planners adhere to such an "environmental deterministic" philosophy of urban problems is not without foundation, and it is the purpose of this section to explore the roots of such a philosophy.

Many books on planning boast that urban planning is a very old profession, since some of the earliest cities on record were planned. One widely used city planning textbook begins with a discussion of cave dwellings and then goes on to examine the early Egyptian and Babylonian cities.[1] Cities such as Kahun (3000 B.C.) and Babylon (2100 B.C.) were laid out according to a plan, and Babylon was even said to have had a building code so stringent that the penalty for gross violations was sometimes death.[2] The roots of planning can next be traced to the classical cities of Rome and Greece, the medieval European cities, the renaissance cities of Europe, and finally the colonial towns of America. The planning texts' discussion of such early cities focuses on the fact that the physical layout of these cities was organized according to some kind of plan.[3] Planning today has been influenced by early town-building in two ways. Most importantly, the planners' concern with early town design has promoted a

---

[1]Arthur B. Gallion and Simon Eisner, *The Urban Pattern: City Planning and Design* (2nd ed.; Princeton: D. VanNostrand Company, Inc., 1963), pp. 3-11.

[2]*Ibid.*, p. 10.

[3]For a detailed history of town design see: Frederick R. Hiorns, *Town Building in History* (London: Harrap, 1956); an excellent study of town design in the United States has been written by John Reps, *The Making of Urban America* (Princeton: Princeton University Press, 1965); for other discussions of early town design see: Gallion and Eisner, *op. cit.*; Christopher Tunnard and Henry Hope Reed, *American Skyline* (New York: Mentor Books, 1956); E. A. Gutkind, *International History of City Development: Urban Development in Central Europe*, Vol. I (New York: Free Press, 1964); *Urban Development in the Alpine and Scandinavian Countries*, Vol. II (New York: The Free Press of Glencoe, Inc., 1965); *Urban Development in Southern Europe: Spain and Portugal* (New York: The Free Press of Glencoe, Inc., 1967).

physical emphasis in planning. Secondly, the actual physical design of early cities has had considerable influence over the design concepts being employed today. Because of the influence of these early planning efforts, it is important to discuss briefly the development of certain town-building concepts.

The cities of antiquity were built in a manner that reflected the culture of the times. Many of the earliest cities were developed for the purpose of protection and were surrounded by a wall. The citadel, a small fortress in which the king lived and the food was kept, was located in the center of these cities. Around the citadel the streets were laid out in a grid pattern in order to house a maximum number of people within the walls of the city. The classical cities of Rome and Greece stressed internal public events much more than protection, emphasizing a civic center, including a forum or agora, and many public buildings. In the ancient cities the scale of the walls and citadel was gigantic in order to glorify the deity-king. The more democratic classical cities, on the other hand, were built to a scale that was much more human, reflecting the greater value placed on the common man. As the classical western civilization began its descent into the Dark Ages, the nature of western cities also underwent a change. Again, cities were walled for protection much as they had been in the earlier period, but the medieval city was built around the church, which was the focus of urban life. Many medieval towns were exceptionally well designed, reflecting the craftsmanship and sense of art possessed by a high percentage of the people. The medieval city placed considerable emphasis on site selection, the relationship between buildings of different sizes and shapes, and the materials for constructing buildings, which resulted in the overall effect of a sculptured townscape.[4]

During the Renaissance period, urban design underwent a further change. While the renaissance city took different forms in different European countries, cities built between the 16th century and the Industrial Revolution were more formal than the medieval city. Stress was placed on long straight avenues; spaces were symmetrical and utilized the horizontal and verticle axis; the gridiron and radial street patterns became popular at this time. These forms were the basis for the pattern of cities as we know them today. The physical structure of the earliest cities in the United States reflected the European town-building concepts which emerged during the Renaissance period.

Two forces were behind the development of many early American cities. One impetus was the need to settle colonists and pioneers as

[4]See Gallion and Eisner, *op. cit.*, Chapter 3, for a discussion of the medieval city.

efficiently as possible. In addition, many communities were developed by land speculators who had purchased great amounts of virgin lands.[5] There were numerous planned communities which never got beyond the land speculator's imagination. Plats of many communities were established and lots were sold sight unseen, but when the settlers arrived, they sometimes found only wilderness. However, there are numerous examples of pre-planned colonial communities that were built and have since prospered. Philadelphia, with its grid street pattern and occasional squares, is today essentially the way it was planned in 1692 by William Penn. James Oglethorpe laid out and built Savannah, Georgia, in 1773. Washington, D.C., with its circular and radial streets overlying a grid pattern, was originally designed by L'Enfant in 1791. The important point about these planned colonial communities is that the influence of the European renaissance city and the motives of land speculation and efficient settlement established urban patterns in the United States that planners must work with today. Furthermore, these early efforts established a tradition in which city planners are basically concerned with the physical environment.

Aside from these early forms of physical city planning, other events which occurred after most of our major cities had been developed contributed to an emphasis on physical design. As the 19th century came to an end, cities in both America and Europe were a product of the Industrial Revolution, and many were crowded, dirty and noisy. The industrial boom that began during the 19th century had made the cities very unpleasant places. Because of the sudden abundance of jobs in cities, the diminishing number of agricultural jobs, and immigration, the United States was changing from a rural to an urban nation. Cities had grown at fantastic rates without the benefit of any guidelines or rules concerning the way development and building ought to proceed. It has been suggested that modern city planning began when people started looking for a way to undo what the Industrial Revolution had done and to prevent a reoccurrence of the haphazard development the 19th century city reflected.[6]

Planning as a function of local government began in the early 20th century, stimulated by the wretched condition of cities. The kinds of solutions to the dirt, noise, and congestion of the city proposed by our first planners consisted of physical alterations in the urban structure.

---

[5]These points are discussed by John Reps, *op. cit.*

[6]Robert A. Walker, *The Planning Function in Urban Government* (2nd ed.; Chicago: University of Chicago Press, 1950), pp. 5-6; Roy Lubove, *The Progressives and the Slums* (Pittsburgh: University of Pittsburgh Press, 1962), Chapter 8.

In fact, these proposed remedies implied that physical alterations in the city would help solve not only the cities' physical problems, but those of a social and economic nature as well.[7]

Some of the earliest proposals to cure the city of its ills came out of the tenement reform movement in New York City. Many citizens deplored the extensive slums that were a product of the Industrial Revolution. Some of those who wished to solve the slum housing problem feared the health hazards created by the slums and the possible harm the slum dweller could do to the rest of the population. These people saw slum removal as a method of social control. Others were more concerned with the effect of the slums on the people who had to live in them, and took the environmental determinist view that the physical condition of the slums was the cause of antisocial behavior and most aspects of human misery.[8] The housing reform movement had its beginning in New York City under the leadership of Jacob Riis at first, and later Lawrence Veiller. Through their efforts, the Tenement Housing Acts of 1867 and 1901 were enacted. Veiller was the founder of modern housing codes, and he was largely responsible for creating the first legislation setting minimum standards for the condition of housing. In addition, Veiller helped establish the machinery to enforce this legislation. Veiller's work is thus the basis for most standards legislation and enforcement machinery that is being used by planners today.[9] Planners were also coming into their own at this time and were working hand-in-hand with housing reformers. Both groups believed that better housing would provide the slum dwellers with a set of values which would be acceptable to everyone.[10] In short, the housing reform movement reflected an environmental determinist philosophy which was widely accepted and used by later planners as they carried out further housing reforms.

The first tenement housing act was passed in New York City in 1867, and it was followed by a more extensive act in 1901. Between the first and second tenement acts another development occurred which also influenced the thinking of planners. The Chicago Fair of 1893 presented to the United States a sharp contrast between what cities of that time were and what they might be. Architects Daniel H. Burnham and Frederick Law Olmsted created a lavish "white city" in

---

[7]Roy Lubove, *op. cit.*, pp. xiv, 246, 255; Lowden Wingo, *Cities and Space: The Future Use of Urban Land* (Baltimore: The Johns Hopkins Press, 1963), pp. 4-5.

[8]*Ibid.*, p. xiv.

[9]Lubove's book contains a detailed description of the housing reform movement in New York. *Ibid.*

[10]*Ibid.*, p. 252.

Chicago's Jackson Park which represented a revival of classical style architecture and town design. Stress was placed on great malls surrounded by grandiose classical buildings. Wide tree-lined boulevards were also used to create an environment that was quite different from the dirty congested 19th century city. The "white city" began a City Beautiful Movement that touched communities across the United States and which gained strength because of the strong distaste of most people for the multitude of problems which were facing cities during this period. Rather than attacking these problems directly, however, an attempt was made to cover them up by a highly superficial beautification process. City Beautiful was, in fact, another manifestation of the environmental determinist approach to urban problem solving. Burnham and Olmsted believed their plans would be the cities' salvation.

For a short period of time enthusiasm over the Chicago Fair and the magnificent "white city" ran high. Many cities actually implemented some of Burnham's proposals. Cleveland, for example, built a civic center on the lakefront according to a Burnham plan. St. Louis also developed a civic center around a wide boulevard complete with parks and fountains, and other cities undertook similar projects. The City Beautiful Movement had its greatest impact between 1900 and 1915, but by 1920 the movement had undergone a shift in emphasis, which has been referred to as "city efficient" or "city useful."[11] The "city efficient" advocates rejected the grandiose schemes of Burnham and his associates in favor of more practical plans which dealt with problems of dirt, congestion, and slums directly. Many engineers who were concerned with the practical problems of public health and the efficient movement of the automobile entered the planning profession. Lack of beauty did not bother the new utilitarian planners as much as the other problems which the city faced.[12] City efficient was not a departure from the emphasis on physical rearrangement as a solution to urban problems. The physical design bias was still there; only the emphasis of that design changed.

As the City Beautiful Movement was gaining momentum in the United States, another approach to planning was beginning in England. In 1898, a young court reporter named Ebenezer Howard published a book called *Tomorrow* in which he outlined the basic ingredients of his conception of garden cities.[13] The garden city idea

---

[11] John Reps, *op. cit.*, p. 524.

[12] Roy Lubove, *op. cit.*, pp. 219-220.

[13] Ebenezer Howard, *Tomorrow: A Peaceful Path to Real Reform* (London: 1898). A third edition came out in 1902 under the title *Garden Cities of Tomorrow*. A revised edition is now available. Ebenezer Howard, *Garden Cities of Tomorrow* (Cambridge: Massachusetts Institute of Technology Press, 1965).

turned into a major planning movement both in England and the United States. Eventually Howard's scheme became embodied in the famous British new towns that surround London today. In the United States some experimental new towns were built during the depression era and others are being built today. The garden city idea has undoubtedly been one of the most powerful influences on modern planning. The planning concepts that came out of this movement will be discussed in detail later in this chapter. At this point we will emphasize the fact that garden cities or new towns are within the tradition of focusing on physical design as a solution to the problems of the 19th century city.

Howard's approach was quite different from anything that had come before it. He believed that most of the problems of the industrial city stemmed from overcrowding and the fact that these cities had been allowed to become too large. The cure for this disease was to create garden cities outside of London where people would live and work which would be limited in size, both in terms of population and area. A publicly owned greenbelt would surround the garden city in order to protect it from encroaching urban development and to make certain the city itself would not sprawl outward. Howard believed the implementation of his idea would result in a decentralization of population from London. Thus, the Howard plan was aimed at creating planned communities and at the same time solving London's problems by halting its spread and lowering its population density. Although unique in its idea of decentralization, the garden city still was based on the assumption that the physical character of the city was at the root of the problems large cities were facing. This assumption reinforced the physical bias of earlier planning movements and hence greatly added to this aspect of the planner's heritage.[14]

At the turn of the century, planners were in general agreement that the physical structure of the 19th century city must be changed, but

---

[14]The garden city idea has been discussed at length in a number of writings. Among the many champions of Howard's ideas and the subsequent applications of them are Lewis Mumford and Frederick Law Olmsted. Both Mumford and Olmsted have written evaluations of the Howard book that appear in the front of the 1965 edition of *Garden Cities of Tomorrow, op. cit.* Also see Lewis Mumford, *The Culture of Cities* (New York: Harcourt, Brace and Company, 1938), pp. 394-401. Raymond Unwin, another strong supporter of Howard, actually designed the first new town of Letchworth. He later became a major figure in the New Towns Movement. For a collection of his essays see: Walter L. Creese, *The Legacy of Raymond Unwin: A Human Pattern for Planning* (Cambridge: The M. I. T. Press, 1967). For a contrary view of the garden city idea see: Jane Jacobs, *The Death and Life of Great American Cities* (New York: Vintage Books, 1963), pp. 17-25.

the legal means for controlling and changing the physical characteristics of the city did not exist in the United States. Beginning about 1860, the cities of Germany began adopting zoning ordinances to control the growth of the medieval German cities. German zoning separated cities into separate zones for different land uses, regulated the height of buildings, and governed the extent to which lots could be covered by these buildings. Planners in the United States saw zoning as a tool that could control land speculation, property value fluctuations, overcrowding, and the future development of urbanized areas generally.[15] As a result, the concept of zoning was accepted by planners and housing reformers with great enthusiasm.

The first zoning ordinance in the United States was adopted by New York City in 1916 through the efforts of a coalition of planners, reformers, and businessmen.[16] George McAneny, President of the Borough of Manhattan; two attorneys, Edward M. Bassett and Lawson Purdy; and Lawrence Veiller were the originators of zoning in New York City.[17] Since 1916 zoning has become the planner's biggest business and consumes a major portion of his time. Practically every major city in the country now has a zoning ordinance. The enthusiasm with which the planner greeted the new zoning tool and the extent to which it is now being used strengthened the physical emphasis of the planning function.

As American cities began to experiment with zoning, planners were also beginning to seek an identity as a professional group. One manifestation of this new professional identity was the First National Planning Conference, held in Washington, D.C., in 1909, which was instigated by New York City housing reformers and was basically geared toward their interests.[18] These particular reformers were interested in utilizing the planners' professional expertise to achieve social and economic goals.[19] The suggested means of achieving these goals were still basically physical: planners were urged to make detailed social and economic surveys to be used as a basis for deciding the most appropriate utilization of physical space. The emphasis on solving social and economic problems was something of a departure from the planners' previous concern. The group sponsoring this

[15]Roy Lubove, *op. cit.*, pp. 229-231.

[16]*Ibid.*, p. 237.

[17]A complete history of zoning in New York City may be found in Stanislaw J. Makielski, Jr., *The Politics of Zoning* (New York: Columbia University Press, 1966).

[18]Robert A. Walker, *op. cit.*, pp. 10-11.

[19]*Ibid.*

conference, however, was not composed primarily of planners and they later formed the National Housing Association.[20]

Another National Planning Conference, sponsored by professional planners, was held in 1910 in Rochester, New York. This conference is generally recognized as the official beginning of the planning movement. It was sponsored by the American Institute of Architects and the American Society of Landscape Architects, among others.[21] During the conference considerable emphasis was placed on the promotion of the City Beautiful Movement. In a sense, this was a rejection of the earlier meeting which had advocated a unified attack on all urban problems, since those attending the National Planning Conference were concerned almost entirely with the concepts of city beautification developed by Burnham and his associates during the Chicago Fair.

Further insight into the strength of planning's physical tradition can be gained by looking at the training of planners during the early 1900's. According to Walker, almost all planners were trained in either architecture or engineering. Walker also suggests that up until the time of the great depression, the physical approach to urban problems completely dominated the planning function in local government. Generally, local governments performed the hardware services such as public works almost to the exclusion of the soft services involving social welfare, with the exception of public safety and health.[22] Thus it is not difficult to understand why the physical emphasis of planning was able to get such a firm grip on the profession. Social or economic planners would not have been acceptable to the prevailing governmental philosophy of the times. Further, the main proponents of planning came from professions which were geared toward a physical approach to urban problems.

Walker has argued that planning began to take a broader approach during and after the great depression, when the hardships of that period created a greater awareness of social and economic problems.[23] Federal programs designed to stimulate the economy brought planners into the business of slum redevelopment and public housing and established welfare as a major governmental function. It is true that changes brought on by the depression ultimately led to

---

[20]*Ibid.*, p. 12.

[21]*Ibid.*, pp. 12-16.

[22]*Ibid.*, pp. 17-36. The term "welfare" is used here to refer to all public services which benefit individuals directly.

[23]*Ibid.*, pp. 36-47.

broader planning concepts. As we will note in a later chapter, the evolution of urban programs financed by the federal government has been a powerful force in creating a greater emphasis on the social sciences in planning. On the other hand, it is also true that many of the federal programs which grew out of the depression provided funds for public works. An analysis of the effect of the depression on planning in the New York City area led one observer to suggest that the influence of the depression was two-fold.[24] In the first place, the depression restricted the scope of ongoing planning operations. Public and private funds which had previously been allocated to planning in New York were curtailed during the depression. Secondly, those funds that were available for planning came primarily from the federal government and they were earmarked for public works projects. For these reasons nearly all planning in New York during the depression was done by engineers and architects who were trained to implement the public works programs being funded. In the case of the Regional Plan Association of New York (a very influential private planning organization), there was a shift of power at the time of the depression from individuals who were concerned with broader aspects of the problems of New York City to those whose interests were focused on physical design. Thus, the immediate impact of the depression in New York was a narrowing of the concept of planning.[25]

In the long run, Walker's point is valid; the depression actually helped broaden the conception of planning to include some concern about the social and economic aspects of urban problems. The broadening process was mainly a result of the evolution of governmental programs which began at the time of the depression. The immediate result of both the depression and the early federal programs, however, was to strengthen the narrower conception of planning through the allocation of the bulk of planning funds to physical projects.

Planners and Ideal Communities

The physical emphasis is only a part of the planner's heritage. Another part is actually a special application of that emphasis: the planning profession's traditional association with the development of "ideal" communities. As mentioned previously, planning possesses

---

[24] Forbes B. Hays, *Community Leadership: The Regional Plan Association of New York* (New York: Columbia University Press, 1965).

[25] *Ibid.*, p. 61.

very little theory that can be used as a basis for the development of land use standards. For this reason planners have relied upon standards derived from a number of "ideal" community designs. The "ideal" community is actually a special type of utopia, but a utopian community is involved with a broader range of subject matter than an "ideal" community under the present usage of these terms. The distinction between utopian and ideal communities has been made by Thomas Reiner, who suggests that while both terms refer to conceptions of a "good place," utopias are concerned basically with the "good" and ideal communities with the "place."[26] Put another way, the ideal community is the planner's conception of utopia and is primarily a physical representation of that utopia.

Because they are closely related, the broader utopian conceptions have had some influence on the planners' more specific ideal communities. America has a rich heritage of utopian conceptions of the "good place." Many of these were focused on religious and/or economic values, and often the utopian thinkers found it necessary to create separate physical communities to achieve their ideals.[27] Among the religious groups that built cities in which the ideals of their orders were the community focus were the Harmonists, Moravians, Shakers, and Mormons. In some instances these communities were established to escape religious persecution; in other cases the separate communities were established in order to experiment with certain social and economic living patterns that could not be implemented in a regular community context. John Humphrey Noyes, for example, founded the community of Oneida, New York, on the principle of a "perfectionist" religion which saw perfection as a function of communistic living arrangements. The Noyes' brand of communism was of the purest order involving the sharing of everything. Marriage in the conventional sense did not exist, but couples practiced a system of rotating free love and the children became community property. All of this was thoroughly justified on religious grounds through a complex theology devised by Noyes.

---

[26]Thomas A. Reiner, *The Place of the Ideal Community in Urban Planning* (Philadelphia: University of Pennsylvania Press, 1963), p. 17.

[27]For a description of most of the more famous American utopian communities see: Mark Holloway, *Heavens on Earth* (London: Turnstile Press, 1951); also, William Alfred Hinds, *American Communities* (New York: Corinth Books, Inc., 1961). John Reps, *op. cit.*, also includes some discussion of these communities in his book. For an interesting discussion of utopian communities from the perspective of professional planning see: John L. Gann, "Cities of Inspiration: Utopian Community Plans and the Pursuit of an Ideal," (Unpublished Master's thesis, Department of Urban and Regional Planning, University of Wisconsin, Madison, Wisconsin, 1967).

The religious communities and those which were simply communistic or socialistic placed almost no emphasis on the physical design of the town. For this reason, they are not directly related to the planners' "ideal" communities. The tradition, however, of setting up communities to develop group goals undoubtedly did encourage the use of the "ideal" community as a means of establishing planning objectives outside of the context of the cities which were already developed.

A link between the utopian and "ideal" communities was the development of company-owned industrial towns. About the time that the labor movement was beginning to gather momentum, many industrialists envisioned establishing industrial towns which would create an ideal environment for a peaceful and prosperous economic enterprise. The founders of Gary, Indiana, for example, were convinced that by isolating the labor force from other workers, by taking them away from other sources of employment, and by providing the workers with all the community facilities they needed, labor trouble could be avoided.[28] The physical structure of Gary reflected the profit oriented value system of its founders. The housing of the workers was very densely populated and was physically situated to maximize accessibility to the industrial plants. Pullman, Illinois, was somewhat more humanistic in its value orientation because George Pullman was genuinely interested in the welfare of his workers as well as in his profits. His approach was to create a physical community which would cause the workers to establish life style patterns that were consistent with Pullman's middle class values.[29] There was one major difference between these industrial towns and the utopian communities. The founders of Pullman and Gary assumed that by creating a certain kind of physical environment the desired social and economic goals would be achieved. The utopian communities concentrated on the social and economic values directly. Pullman's philosophy of environmental determinism was sharply challenged when he discovered that the life style of his workers was not altered by the new environment. He attempted to force the issue by levying fines for such offenses as poor housekeeping or sitting on the porch steps wearing an undershirt.[30] Such paternalism eventually led to disillusionment, strike and violence. While planners were among those to damn Pullman for

---

[28] John Reps, *op. cit.*, p. 5.

[29] Stanley Buder, "The Model Town of Pullman: Town Planning and Social Control in the Gilded Age," *Journal of the American Institute of Planners* (January, 1967), p. 3.

[30] *Ibid.*, p. 7.

his paternalistic actions, it did not shake the planning profession's faith in the importance of the physical environment or of ideal communities. Most planners would still agree that physically the town of Pullman, Illinois, incorporated the best traditions of planning.

The development of utopian and company-owned industrial towns in America laid the foundation for accepting ideal communities as a basis for location and space standards which could be used in many city plans. There is a long list of ideal communities which may have influenced the planning standards being used today.[31]

Among the many ideal communities which have made contributions to today's planning standards, Ebenezer Howard's "garden city," Clarence Stein and Henry Wright's "new towns," and Clarence Perry's "neighborhood unit" have, in the author's judgment, been the most significant.[32]

As discussed earlier, Ebenezer Howard was an Englishman who sought to solve London's problems by establishing a ring of economically and socially independent towns around the London complex.[33] Although Howard drew diagrams of the physical layout of his garden city, he made it quite clear that these diagrams should not be taken literally. He did intend, however, that the planning standards implied by his diagrams and the garden city concept should become a basis for future city planning. Howard's design depicted London surrounded by a ring of cities which were connected by major highways. Each garden city was surrounded by a publicly owned greenbelt which would keep the cities from spreading into one another. Within the city he used a radial street pattern with homes of different densities and different land uses separated from one another by buffers of parks and/or highways.

Many of the planning standards developed in Howard's garden city have been widely used by planners as a basis for physical land use standards. Howard assumed that bigness (both in terms of area and population) was at the root of city problems, so his major thesis was that planned decentralization was the key to the elimination of urban disorder. The actual building of the British new towns was a very real indication that this view enjoyed wide acceptance among

---

[31]Thomas Reiner has done a detailed analysis of twenty ideal communities. Students wishing to explore the ideal community's contribution to planning in greater depth should read the Reiner study, *op. cit.*

[32]Significance in this context is the author's subjective judgment that the propositions derived from the communities have been used more than the propositions derived from other communities.

[33]Ebenezer Howard, *op. cit.* Howard's work is evaluated as an ideal community by Reiner, *op. cit.*, pp. 39-43.

British planners and the public generally.[34] In the United States, planners have long been in substantial agreement that the decentralization approach is correct. During the depression, American planners were successful in selling the federal government on the idea of building new towns. Thus, "greenbelt" towns such as Greenhills, Ohio, and Greenbelt, Maryland, were constructed but they were not really related to metropolitan areas nor did they use public ownership of land to control growth. More recently, considerable pressure has been placed on Congress to pass legislation which would provide government assistance for the establishment of a new towns program. In a number of places new towns are being constructed once again with private money. Reston, Virginia, outside of Washington, is one of the most famous examples. Howard's thesis that planned decentralization is the appropriate approach to solve our urban problems has had a substantial impact on the development of modern planning practice.

Related to the decentralization thesis are several ideas that are also widely accepted by planners, such as the limited size concept. A number of economists have struggled with the theoretical position that there is an optimum size for cities, but nothing substantial has come out of this struggle. Howard suggested 32,000 as the maximum size for his cities; others have suggested different sizes. There is a lack of criteria for deciding what size is optimum, and no real evidence establishing a causal connection between size and problems. Nevertheless, the limited size concept has many adherents. Closely related to limited size is limited density. Not only were Howard and his followers convinced that size caused problems, but they also wished to keep densities low.[35] Evidence that the elimination of high density will solve our urban ills is also lacking. Yet the limited density concept is widely accepted and has become a basis for the land use standards in many plans.

The use of publicly owned open space to control development and enhance aesthetic appeal was another of Howard's innovations. This practice was in part a logical extension of some of Howard's other ideas. A greenbelt of open land around the garden city was used to control both density and town growth. All greenbelts and parks were to be publicly owned (as was all land in the garden city) so that an

---

[34]For a general history and evaluation of British new towns see: Frederic J. Osborn and Arnold Whittick, *The New Towns: The Answer to Megalopolis* (New York: McGraw Hill Book Co., 1963).

[35]Raymond Unwin, "Nothing Gained by Overcrowding!" in Creese, *op. cit.*, pp. 109-126.

open space policy could be enforced. Like Howard's other concepts, this policy has been widely accepted by most of today's planners, and has become a basis for land use standards.

A final proposition in the Howard scheme that has found wide acceptance was the separation of different land uses. Although Howard does not go into any great detail over the reasons for the separations he made, he did suggest that most of his locations were based on the practical considerations of traffic generation and land use compatibility. While the idea of separating the land uses may not have been original with Howard, it was incorporated into his scheme. This idea has traditionally been a very important basis for locating land uses in city plans. Although a few modern plans are moving away from rigid land use separations, many more seem to adhere to the traditional views.

One of the important applications of the Howard scheme in the United States was Radburn, New Jersey. The designers of Radburn, Clarence Stein and Henry Wright, were followers of Ebenezer Howard.[36] Their design incorporated many of the concepts outlined above; but it added a few elements that have received considerable attention by planners. Stein and Wright eliminated through traffic on residential streets by the use of culs-de-sac and large blocks termed "superblocks," in which homes were turned away from the streets and oriented toward a large continuous tract of open space.[37] The assumption behind these innovations was that less through traffic and more open space would establish a more interesting and pleasant residential community. The "superblock" idea has become another important basis for the design of cities.

Another "ideal" community scheme that has been a significant influence on the establishment of land use standards is Clarence Perry's neighborhood unit analysis.[38] In the 1929 survey of the New York metropolitan area, Perry argued that using the neighborhood unit as the basic planning area could restore a sense of community to

---

[36]Clarence Stein, *Toward New Towns for America* (New York: Reinhold Publishing Corporation, 1956).

[37]Neither the cul-de-sac nor the superblock were original with Stein and Wright. They were influenced by Unwin's designs for some of the British new towns where he used both. The superblock had also been introduced earlier at an exhibition in Berlin in 1911. But Stein and Wright did introduce these ideas to the United States. Their real innovation was to use these design concepts to create a community which would be compatible with the automobile age.

[38]Clarence Perry, *The Neighborhood Unit*, Vol. 7, *Neighborhood and Community Planning* (New York: Regional Survey of New York and Its Environs, 1929).

large metropolitan areas and that the planning of future residential communities should emphasize the neighborhood and make it physically distinct. Detailed physical guidelines for neighborhood units were established based on a number of assumptions.[39] Perry believed that social interaction was an essential part of urban life and that such interaction was at least partially a function of the nature of the physical environment. The standards used for the physical environment were derived from a variety of sources. Perry's "ideal" neighborhood was limited in size to an area that would support one elementary school with an enrollment of 1,000. Density was to be kept to ten persons per acre in an area of about 160 acres. At the center of the neighborhood was an elementary school-community center, some churches, and a few shops. Major shopping areas were to be located at the periphery of the unit, and the street pattern was designed to keep all through traffic out. In essence, Perry advocated the creation of a small unit where all residents could walk to the community facilities (maximum of a half mile) and where opportunities for neighborhood interaction would be maximized by the lack of traffic and the presence of a community center.

Although there has been some disagreement over the details of Perry's neighborhood concept, the proposition that the neighborhood ought to be the planning unit and the assumptions behind this proposition have been widely accepted by planners.[40] In fact, much of the detail of Perry's original proposal has been accepted at face value and incorporated into many plans. Many of the institutions which have great influence over the planning function have either advocated or required the use of the neighborhood concept in residential planning. The federal government requires a neighborhood analysis as a prerequisite for urban renewal funds. The Urban Land Institute has incorporated the neighborhood concept into their handbook on community building. The neighborhood idea is used by the American Public Health Association as a basis for healthful housing standards. There is also evidence that organizations such as Federal Housing Authority and Mortgage Bankers Association use the neighborhood

---

[39]Thomas Reiner, *op. cit.*, pp. 62-63.

[40]Much of the disagreement over Perry's definition of the neighborhood unit centers around the question of whether the residents should be of similar socioeconomic composition. See Lawrence Haworth, *The Good City* (Bloomington: Indiana University Press, 1963), pp. 106-129; Howard W. Hallman, "Citizens and Professionals Reconsider the Neighborhood," *Journal of the American Institute of Planners* (August, 1959), pp. 121-127; Herbert J. Gans, "The Balanced Community: Homogeneity or Heterogeneity in Residential Areas?" *Journal of the American Institute of Planners* (May, 1961), pp. 176-184.

concept as a basis for judging the soundness of residential areas.[41] Taking the conceptions of Howard, Stein, and Perry together, it is quite clear how much the "ideal" community is a part of the planners' heritage. Planned decentralization, limited size, limited density, greenbelts, separation of land uses, "superblocks" and the neighborhood unit concept are all key planning propositions that have been derived from the physical utopias we have called ideal communities.

Bosses, Reformers and Planners

One final aspect of the planners' heritage involves his attitude toward government. Planners have traditionally distrusted local government, viewing it as the pawn of special interest groups. This distrust is at least partly the result of the relationship between the planning movement and the municipal reform movement. Earlier we noted that the planning movement began as a reaction to the physical condition of the 19th century city, but the founders of the planning movement were also concerned about the governmental condition of the city. At the turn of the century, many cities were being run by machine organizations which were believed to be corrupt and inefficient. Large numbers of individuals in different cities began a municipal reform movement designed to "throw the rascals out." The municipal reform movement and the planning movement occurred simultaneously, and planners tended to share a similar set of attitudes with municipal reformers about the evils of machine politics and the way cities ought to be run. These early conceptions of politics are a very important component of the planners' heritage. Planners developed a general aversion to "politics." Politicians were stereotyped using the machine boss as a model.

Although the nature of city government has changed, the negative attitudes formed during an earlier period have persisted. Planners have sometimes rejected association with city government entirely and have attempted to operate independent of it. A concrete

---

[41]For an indication of the extent of the acceptance of the Perry Neighborhood Unit Concept, see the following influential planning textbooks: Donald H. Webster, *Urban Planning and Municipal Public Policy* (New York: Harper and Row Publishers, 1958), pp. 144-145; Arthur B. Gallion and Simon Eisner, *The Urban Pattern, op. cit.*, pp. 250-264; Mary McLean, ed., *Local Planning Administration* (Chicago: International City Managers Association, 1959), pp. 112-122. Also see, American Public Health Association, *Planning the Neighborhood* (Chicago: Public Administration Service, 1948); Urban Land Institute, *The Community Builders Handbook* (Washington: Urban Land Institute, 1960), pp. 77-155.

manifestation of this attempt is the semi-independent planning commission through which most planning agencies operate today. These commissions were designed to be immune to the meddling of corrupt politicians and special interests.

While many planners are beginning to recognize that "politics" is not all evil and that it is, in fact, a necessary component of planning decision-making, others still cling to the old view. An understanding of their distrust of government requires a knowledge of the nature of machine politics, the municipal reform movement, and the ultimate demise of the machine.

By the turn of the century most major cities in the United States were governed by machine organizations. While political machines took slightly different forms in different cities, there are certain characteristics that were common to the political machine style of politics generally.[42] The political machine was in the business of exchanging favors for votes. This exchange took place within a highly centralized organization which lacked ideology and was basically interested in self-perpetuation. The boss, who was at the top of the chain of command, was served by a number of ward leaders who were responsible for distributing the favors and collecting the votes. Each ward leader, in turn, had a staff of precinct captains who made most of the initial contacts with the voters. Precinct captains and ward leaders were generally chosen by some elected party official and given an appointed job by the party which would allow them to have a reasonable income while pursuing their major work for the party. The ultimate objective of this work was to deliver the votes on election day. This was a full time job, which required frequent visits to the neighbors, doing various tasks for the party and generally being available to the voters. For the most part, the precinct captains and ward leaders asked individuals to exchange their votes for tokens of friendship, although cash, coal, or turkeys at Christmas time were occasionally given to the loyal electorate.

The fact that large numbers of individuals were willing to trade their vote for such a seemingly meager award has mystified the

---

[42]There are numerous discussions of these characteristics available. The discussion in this volume is based upon the following sources. Edward C. Banfield and James Q. Wilson, *City Politics* (Cambridge, Mass.: Harvard University Press, 1965), pp. 115-121; Edward C. Banfield, ed., *Urban Government: A Reader in Administration and Politics* (New York: The Free Press of Glencoe, Inc., 1961), pp. 132-190; *The Annals of the American Academy of Political and Social Science: City Bosses and Political Machines* (May, 1964); James Bryce, *The American Commonwealth* (New York: G. P. Putnam's Sons, 1959), pp. 183-217.

reformers. It is apparent that the voters on whom the machine depended for its support held a very different set of values than those who viewed the machine operations with horror. The machine did distribute jobs on the basis of party loyalty, offer bribes, and profit by graft, but these activities did not bother a substantial segment of the community. The apparent differences in values could be explained by the fact that the machine fulfilled certain functions which many reformers overlooked.[43] Machine politics provided services to immigrants in a personalized manner that could not be matched by impersonal welfare workers. Poor people looked to the precinct captain as a friend to whom they could go for help when they needed it, and during the height of machine politics there was no other organization that could fulfill this function. At the same time the machine offered a means of social mobility to lower income groups, for although the conventional avenues toward social and economic advancement were ordinarily blocked during the 19th and early 20th centuries, the machine provided jobs and prestige for individuals who probably could not have "made it" any other way. The machine also performed services for business. At the turn of the century the economy was booming, cities were being developed, and there were fortunes to be made by businessmen by seeking special favors and dispensations from the political system. Businessmen desired certainty in the relationship between the public and the private sector. The machine granted this certainty, along with business favors such as street and railroad franchises and contracts for street paving, public buildings, or other construction, in return for their support.[44]

Thus the machine performed certain functions for the populace of cities and in return this populace gave the machine its vote. Obviously, it was a necessary condition of this kind of transaction for the majority of voters in the city to value their vote less than the functions which the machine performed. Banfield and Wilson have suggested that people of the working class, especially immigrants, do not value their vote as much as do other groups of people.[45] The importance of the vote must be measured relative to those things which are offered in return for that vote. In the case of low-income immigrants, the importance of the vote was undoubtedly low relative to the considerable inducements which the machine could offer them.

---

[43]Robert K. Merton, "The Latent Functions of the Machine," in Edward C. Banfield, ed., *op. cit.*, pp. 180-190.

[44]Fred I. Greenstein, "The Changing Pattern of Urban Party Politics," *The Annals of the American Academy of Political and Social Science* (May, 1964), p. 4.

[45]Banfield and Wilson, *op. cit.*, pp. 118-119.

Graft and bribery were offensive to the middle- and upper-income reformers, so they began to do what they could to end the system. Reformer-journalist Lincoln Steffens saw the workings of machine politics in the early 1900's as "the shame of the cities." He thought that by publicizing the "shameful facts" he could "burn through our civic shamelessness and set fire to American pride."[46] Other reformers of this era have stated that it is the "politics" in government that is bad. One critic has suggested, for example, that there is an "evil theory" behind local government.

> What is this evil theory? It is simply that the city is a political body; that its interior affairs have to do with national political parties and issues. My fundamental contention is that a city is a corporation; that as a city it has nothing whatever to do with general political interests, that party political names and duties are utterly out of place here. The questions in a city are not political questions.[47]

A direct contrast to this is the machine politicians' theory of government, exemplified in William Riordon's collection of talks by Tammany politician George Washington Plunkitt.[48] Plunkitt stressed what the machine did for those who were loyal to Tammany. He saw nothing wrong or immoral about the fact that he made millions of dollars from politics. Plunkitt made it his business to find out about the city's plans to develop parks or to build bridges or buildings so that he could buy the appropriate land and materials and sell them to the city at enormous profits. He called this practice "honest graft" and distinguished it from "dishonest graft," which included direct stealing from the city treasury and blackmail. This "dishonest graft" was wrong, but "honest graft" was simply a part of the game. "I seen my opportunities and I took 'em," was Plunkitt's explanation of the fortune he made in politics. Plunkitt displayed the same distaste for the reformers that they had for him, as evidenced in his comments on the civil service.

> This civil service law is the biggest fraud of the age. It is the curse of the nation. There can't be no real patriotism while it lasts. How are

---

[46]Lincoln Steffens, *The Shame of the Cities* (New York: Hill and Wang, 1963), p. 12.

[47]Andrew D. White, "Municipal Affairs are not Political," Edward C. Banfield, *Urban Government*, p. 213.

[48]William L. Riordon, *Plunkitt of Tammany Hall: A Series of Very Plain Talks on Very Practical Politics* (New York: E. P. Dutton & Co., 1963). A detailed account of the careers of twenty machine bosses may be found in: Harold Zink, *City Bosses in the United States* (Durham: Duke University Press, 1930).

you goin' to interest our young men in their country if you have no offices to give them when they work for their party?[49]

White's contention that "politics" should be kept out of city government was just as ridiculous to Plunkitt as Plunkitt's distinction between honest and dishonest graft was to White. Reformers could not understand the appeal of the machine, and the machine could not understand the philosophy of the reformers. Ultimately the reformers prevailed. Remnants of the machine style persist, but the classical machine itself has not survived in American city government. Reformers have been successful in introducing civil service laws, voting machines, nonpartisan elections, at-large elections, city manager governments, and other innovations designed to cut into the source of strength of political machines. Machines fell, however, not so much as a result of these reforms but because of some fundamental changes in American society.[50]

One factor was the halt in the flow of immigration to the United States from European countries, which had been virtually cut off by 1927. The machine had relied heavily on immigrant votes, and the cessation of immigration nearly eliminated the growth of potential machine voters. As the same time, those individuals who had once been immigrants began to assimilate into American society. Friendship and petty favors began to lose their importance to these individuals because they had already achieved a certain amount of upward mobility. The advent of the New Deal programs following the depression also restricted the machine's supply of rewards for the faithful. The institutionalization of welfare programs effectively eliminated personal welfare services from the array of favors dispensed by the machine, and after World War II, rising incomes made such services even less important. The machine's offer of friendship for votes also lost much of its importance as a result of changes in life style and ethnic patterns. The advent of television, for one thing, made visits from the precinct captain more of an interruption than a pleasure. Furthermore, the ethnic composition of the cities began to change. Negroes now lived in homes previously occupied by European ethnic groups which had moved to other parts of the metropolis. The Irish precinct captain, who lacked the understanding of his neighbor's

---

[49]*Ibid.*, p. 12.

[50]These changes are discussed in greater detail in the following sources: Banfield and Wilson, *op. cit.*, pp. 121-125; Fred I. Greenstein, "The Changing Pattern of Urban Party Politics," *op. cit.*; William C. Havard, "From Bossism to Cosmopolitanism: Changes in the Relationship of Urban Leadership," *The Annals of the American Academy of Political and Social Science* (May, 1964), pp. 84-94.

culture he had once had, found it difficult to offer friendship to the Negro. The availability of jobs for patronage purposes began to diminish rapidly as civil service laws became more and more pervasive. Even in the early 1900's Plunkitt was complaining about the civil service laws, and since that time they have become much more important. Thus, the incentives which the machine could offer those willing to give up their vote have been cut into by many external forces.

Although the machine in its classical form is a thing of the past, the ideology that developed as a reaction to machine practices persists. A basic element in the reformist ideology is that there is a public interest that can be applied to all of the issues of local government. The public interest is that course of action which best serves the public as a whole. Private interests, according to the reformist, must take a back seat to the public interest. Many reformists believe that "politics" involves the serving of private interests and should, therefore, be kept out of government. This element of the reformist ideology was an important premise of the planning movement in the United States.

A very basic assumption behind the existence of the planning function of government is that the natural processes of the private market cannot allocate land to uses that benefit the public as a whole. The turn-of-the-century planner saw government at that time as a force on the side of the "irrational" interplay of private interests which had created a city of horrors. Quite obviously, the machine politicians did operate on the principal of satisfying private interests. Thus, it was natural that the planner should ally himself with the municipal reformer who was also dedicated to the ideals of a "good" government which would serve the public interest in an efficient manner.

The concept of the master plan, a blueprint for the development of the city of the future, was a part of the reformist-planner's public interest ideal. Early expressions of fear that this would be corrupted by the immediate and private interest-oriented goals of the politicians were numerous. Tugwell's famous speech advocating a "fourth power" status for planning which would be a notch above the executive, legislative and judicial branches of government was one such expression. Tugwell was concerned with protecting the plan from "disruption and compromise" on the part of elected officials.[51] At the same time that Tugwell was delivering his "fourth power" address to the

---

[51]Charles S. Ascher, "City Planning, Administration and Politics," *Land Economics* (Nov., 1954), pp. 320-328.

American Institute of Planners in Washington, Lewis Mumford was making a similar recommendation to planners in Honolulu. Mumford proposed to appoint a planning director who would have ultimate control over all funds for capital improvements and a longer term of office than any elected official.[52]

Today, few planners would deny the importance of politics in the planning process. The open hostility toward politics which characterized early planning efforts has subsided into a quiet acceptance of the government and its elected officials as necessary to the implementation of plans. While there are no recent polls of the modern planner's attitudes, there is evidence to suggest that many planners today still inwardly harbor many of the old feelings toward politics. Planners still seem to feel that elected officials represent immediate special interests which are by definition at odds with the long range public interests of the planner and that his role in politics is to attempt to persuade the politician to accept the long-run public interest view. Stuart Chapin, for example, implies in his widely-read text that governments are often controlled by a "power structure" which is in the business of subverting the public interest. He sees the "political climate" in a community as a practical consideration in the planning process which is capable of setting a "lower limit" on the extent to which planning controls can be utilized in the public interest.[53] The idea that the planner and not the politician is the true guardian of the public interest is also expressed by Webster in his planning text. He suggests that opposition to "sound policies" may often be the result of organized special interests or lack of understanding. The very fact that a public official must make a choice between sound and unsound policy is the result of a "lack of planning effectiveness."[54] Another planner has written that the mayors and councils are "too busy" to be concerned with future development.[55]

After a thorough examination of the actual operation of the planning process in the Minneapolis-St. Paul area, Alan Altshuler concluded that the planner of today seems to be convinced that it is both ethical and necessary to play the political game.[56] The way in which

---

[52]*Ibid.*, pp. 322-323.

[53]F. Stuart Chapin, Jr., *Urban Land Use Planning* (2nd ed.; Urbana: University of Illinois Press, 1965), pp. 60-62.

[54]Donald H. Webster, *Urban Planning and Municipal Public Policy* (New York: Harper & Row, 1958), p. 6.

[55]John T. Howard, "In Defense of Planning Commissions," *Journal of the American Institute of Planners* (Spring, 1951), pp. 89-94.

[56]Alan Altshuler, *The City Planning Process* (Ithaca: Cornell University Press, 1965), pp. 355-356.

he plays the game, pitting himself against the politicians, is probably at least partially a reflection of his reformist heritage. As Altshuler observes, the planning ideal is still a comprehensive plan which is a reflection of the planner's presumed special knowledge of the public interest.[57] This ideal in practice is often compromised by the desire of the planner to avoid conflict and have his plan accepted. Nevertheless, the ideal persists and the planner of today still sees politics as a subversion of the public oriented goals for which planning stands. While it is not easy to say how much the planner of today is still affected by his reformist roots, it is clear that the old-style politics and the subsequent reform movement are an important ingredient of the planner's heritage.

Conclusion

The planner comes into the planning process with a set of values and procedures that have been strongly influenced by certain events which were a part of the evolution of the planning movement. These events we have called the planners' heritage. Part of this heritage is an environmental deterministic view of urban problems. As planning evolved, a tremendous stress was placed on the physical aspects of the community. The belief that a good physical environment would wipe out the social and economic ills faced by cities and that well conceived physical development would prevent new urban communities from acquiring these problems was the reason for planning's traditional physical orientation. The stress on the physical environment required a set of standards for land use. Such standards have been largely derived from a number of ideal community conceptions. These physical utopias have been a very important part of the planners' heritage because so many of the planning procedures and standards in use today have been taken directly from ideal community propositions. The third aspect of the planners' heritage that has influenced professional values and practices is the association between the planning movement and the municipal reform movement. Many of the municipal reformers' attitudes toward the local government were also held by the planners. The "good government" attitude that shunned "politics" and "politicians" became a part of the planners' bundle of professional attitudes and values. In recent years the planners' conception of "politics" has become slightly more sophisticated. But the

[57] *Ibid.*, p. 299.

suspicious attitude toward government that resulted from the early 20th century exposure to machine politics still lingers on. Thus, an emphasis on physical design, a reliance on physical utopias, and a distrust for local government have been the major manifestations of the planners' heritage.

3 Local Governments and Their Planning Agencies

Our understanding of how a municipal planner performs his service role would be incomplete if we stopped after analyzing his heritage. The planning function of municipal government operates within a governmental context. The governmental context of the planning function should be considered a major variable in the formulation of planning policy. The term "variable" is used here in a literal sense; variations in the governmental context of planning are almost as extensive as the number of planning agencies in existence. For nearly every planning agency there is a unique mixture of governmental programs and responsibilities. These have a significant impact on how the planner is able to serve his community. The particular mixture for a given planning agency may affect planning policy formulation in two ways: first, it affects the kinds of planning issues which arise; second, it will partially determine the route which the planner must take to communicate his ideas to the political decision makers.

The various formal institutional arrangements which define the administrative structure of local planning agencies are numerous. These arrangements have evolved out of the development of the structure of municipalities. Municipalities were originally established by state governments to provide services needed by people living in urban communities. When municipalities were few in number and small in size, the functions which states allowed them to perform were limited. In some instances local public services were initially provided by semi-independent agencies which gradually merged with the municipality. Planning was introduced to municipal government as an agency which was legally separated from the regular municipal government. Planning commissions composed of respected citizens in the community were appointed by public officials to carry on the city planning. In many instances, the commissioners had no budget and served without pay as citizen advisors to the elected municipal officials. Unlike most other municipal functions, a majority of the planning agencies have retained this semi-independent status. Only education has managed to remain more aloof from municipal government than planning. Interestingly enough, in both the education and planning fields, there has been a running debate over the question of the desirability of independence from municipal government. In fact, many of the arguments used by the planners to justify an independent or semi-independent status are identical to those used by the advocates of continued independence for education. Planning has been said to be a special kind of function which serves the public interest and should, therefore, be above "politics." Over the years, some of the arguments have become a little more sophisticated in both the planning and the education debates. Nevertheless, the question of the best organization for the planning function has, for the most part, consisted of a repetition of old arguments. Consideration must be given to these arguments since the position of planning in the structure of local government is an important aspect of planning's governmental context.

A knowledge of the debate is useful in pointing up some of the questions raised by planning agency organization. The debate has not been useful, however, in determining whether an independent planning agency will affect the performance of the planning function differently from an agency which is integrated with the municipal government. The debators have rarely attempted to determine what kind of impact each arrangement has had on planning practice. Instead most of the debate has been based upon the personal experiences of planners. These experiences have been fundamentally different. Even with little data on the planning organization question it is clear that the structural arrangements for the planning function are of significance. The formal linkages between the planner and the policy makers may affect both the kinds of issues which come to the planners' attention and the planners' ability to communicate with other governmental officials. Thus, some knowledge of alternative structural arrangements, the arguments that have been made for and against these arrangements, and some speculations concerning their impact on the planning function are important to our understanding of the formulation of planning policy.

Municipal Governmental Structures

It is interesting to note that many people having lived their lives in a city with a particular form of government, have the impression that all city governments are structured similarly. If the mayor is strong and is the policy initiator in a city, its residents have a tendency to assume that all mayors have this kind of role in city government. Many planners have based their prescriptions for the best planning organization on the structure of municipal government that they have been working or living under. Such assumptions about similarities among municipal governmental structures are fallacious. American municipal government encompasses a number of fundamentally different structural types and within each type a seemingly infinite number of variations. These types and variations refer only to the formal decision making roles and responsibilities. If we were to consider the informal structure of government, the number of different types of municipal governments would be almost as great as the number of existing governments. Since there are so many different formal arrangements, we will describe in general terms only the major structural types. The reader should keep in mind, however, that there is considerable variation within each of the categories described.

One of the oldest forms of municipal government is the *weak* mayor-council type. Under this system the council assumes both executive and administrative roles. The various city departments, such as police, fire, and finance, are run directly by the councilmen through a committee system in which there is a separate council committee for each city department. Department heads are sometimes elected directly by the voters. The mayor under this arrangement, is only an advisor to both the council and the department heads. Although he is an elected official, he has few if any formal powers. The weak mayor-council government has been widely criticized for its inability to separate administrative and legislative duties and for a lack of coordination of governmental activities. Consequently, this once popular form of municipal government is today rare.

A more prevalent type of governmental structure is the *strong* mayor-council. Under this system, both the mayor and the members of the city council are elected by the voters. It is the mayor's responsibility to appoint and/or dismiss all executive officers and administrators. The various city departments are directly under his control. Aside from his administrative duties, the mayor can develop and introduce legislation to the council, and has the power to veto legislation that the council has enacted. The mayor's formal position of central authority and his ability to provide jobs makes him a powerful political figure in city government. The role of the city council is strictly legislative, initiating legislation and enacting it. In many cities, much of the council's time is spent deliberating on legislation that has been proposed by the mayor and his executive officers.

A third type of municipal government, the commission, is found most often in smaller cities. This scheme was developed in Texas in the early 1900's.[1] Its popularity increased as municipal reformers supported it as a more efficient form of government than any yet devised. Like the weak mayor-council, the commission government combines the legislative and executive duties. A number of directly elected commissioners acting as both executive department heads and councilmen provide governmental leadership. One of the commissioners is generally elected as mayor and then serves as mayor, department head, and president of council. The other commissioners are elected at large and their departmental role such as commissioner of fire, police, etc., is decided by the commissioners after the election. Each commissioner is responsible for the appointment or dismissal of those executive officers and administrators within his department. The commissioners propose, enact, and execute all legislation and policy. In terms of formal power, the mayor has no more control over the municipal government than any other commissioner. The mayor's only duties beyond those of the other commissioners involve the coordination of policy. Informal practices, however, sometimes give the mayor additional powers, allowing him to function as a strong executive. The other commissioners then became his staff. Since the commissioners control both legislative and executive activities, power is sometimes more highly centralized under the commission government than under any other type.

The newest major type of municipal organization is the council-manager. The development of this form of government was begun by a group of municipal reformers in 1911. The greatest growth in the adoption of the council-manager plan came during a fifteen year period after the Second World War when approximately seventy-five

---

[1]Charles R. Adrian, *Governing Urban America* (2nd ed.; New York: McGraw-Hill Book Co. Inc., 1961), pp. 214-218.

municipalities a year adopted the system. In more recent years this council-manager boom has cooled off.[2] The major assumption made by advocates of council-manager government is that cities should be run like a business. The objective of city government, however, is not to make profits, but rather to serve the public. The developers of the council-manager plan thought this objective could be accomplished best by centralizing the authority for the formulation of policy in the hands of a small council. All administrative responsibility (the "business" side of government) would be assumed by a professional administrator chosen by the elected council members. Thus, the typical council-manager government consists of an elected council which handles all legislative matters and has ultimate control over the executive function. A professional city manager is appointed by the council. He serves "at the council's pleasure" which means they can fire him at any time. His duties are to take charge of all administrative matters. The theory and practice of council-manager governments cannot always be reconciled. In some cases, the manager has taken an aggressive role by forming key political alignments to prevent his dismissal and then acting more like a strong mayor. In other instances, the manager has been bandied about at the will of the more powerful councilmen.

Planning Agency Organization

All local planning agencies are attached in some way to one of the four major types of municipal governments. Thus, even two planning agencies with similar internal organization may operate quite differently because of differences in the municipal governments to which they are attached. Planning agency organizations vary considerably, however, beyond their relationship to the structure of municipal government. Three major types of planning agency organizations are identified here: the semi-independent planning commission, the executive staff agency, and the legislative staff agency.

As noted earlier, planning made its debut as a semi-independent function. In most communities the semi-independent planning agency still persists, set apart from the rest of the municipal agencies. A

[2]An excellent discussion of the council-manager form may be found in Edward C. Banfield and James Q. Wilson, *City Politics* (Cambridge, Mass.: Harvard University Press and the M. I. T. Press, 1963), pp. 168-186. The material presented here is partly based on this discussion. Also see Charles Adrian, *op. cit.*, pp. 218-30.

planning commission composed of "respected" citizens in the community is appointed by the members of the council, or by one of the department heads; by the mayor with the consent of the council; or the commissioners may be elected. The important point is that in almost all cases a commissioner is very difficult to remove from office once appointed. Formal charges are generally required for dismissal. Further, commission members are usually appointed for overlapping terms. The theory behind these appointment procedures is to insulate the commission members from the influence of the politicians. In the early days of planning commissions, the commissioners themselves generally did the planning. However, in most cities of any size today, the planning commission has at a minimum one full-time planning director who is a trained professional. In more and more cities, the planning director has been given a staff of professionals. Under the purest form of the semi-independent planning agency, the commissioners hire the planning director and his staff. Under such circumstances, the professional planner's client is the planning commission. The professionals make their recommendations to the commissioners who in turn decide what recommendations will be made to the council and/or to the chief executive. Thus, under the semi-independent planning agency, the route from the professional planner's recommendation to implementation involves three steps. First, based on their research and know-how, the professionals make recommendations to the commission. Then the commissioners make recommendations to the executive and the legislative bodies, based on the planners' recommendations and their own citizen's point of view. Finally, the council decides whether to pass legislation or the executive decides what to do about the recommendations of the planning commission. Political and administrative considerations come into the decision at this point. In some instances, the professional planners are appointed by the elected officials (usually the chief executive) to serve both the planning commission and the executive or council. In this case, the professional-client relationship is more complex and the road from professional recommendation to action has a few more curves.

One reason the semi-independent planning commission is still predominant is that this type of organization is imbedded in many state statutes. In order for municipalities to engage in planning, they must have permission from the state government in the form of enabling legislation. In 1928 the United States Department of Commerce published a Standard City Planning Enabling Act which many states used as a model for their planning enabling statutes.[3] Other model acts were the basis for a number of additional state statutes.[4] These early models of state planning legislation have greatly influenced the organization of the planning function. The model acts favored the semi-independent lay planning commission to administer the planning function.

A few states have made their legislation more flexible. Others have granted "home rule" charters to their cities which allow them to organize planning agencies to their own liking. These developments have opened up the opportunity for other forms of planning agency organization. In some municipalities, the planning function has become a regular executive agency. With this arrangement, the planner is hired directly by the mayor or city manager and is responsible to him. The planning commission usually continues to perform its advisory role. The planner and his staff become either a special agency in the office of the mayor or manager or a regular administrative department. They have the same status as police, fire, finance, and all of the other departments. Thus, when the planning function is established as an executive agency, the professional planners' client is the mayor or city manager. Recommendations made by the planner go directly to the chief executive who in turn may make legislative proposals to council or act directly on his planner's advice.

Planning can alternatively be a legislative staff agency where the planners' primary client is the city council. A pure form of this type of organization would eliminate the citizens' planning commission. The professional staff would serve the council directly. However, as in the case of the executive staff agency, the citizens' planning commission can continue to play an important role.[5] The professionals in such an agency still advise the commission but are hired by and are more closely aligned with the city council.

It must be stressed that the planning agency organizations described above are general types. The variations of agency organization within each of these types are very great. Additionally, when we consider the different varieties of municipal governmental structures,

---

[3]U. S. Department of Commerce, *The Standard City Planning Enabling Act* (Washington: U. S. Government Printing Office, 1928).

[4]Edward M. Bassett, *et al.*, *Model Laws for Planning Cities, Counties and States*, Harvard City Planning Studies, Vol. VII (Cambridge: Harvard University Press, 1935).

[5]Berkeley, California, has such an arrangement. Its operations are thoroughly described and evaluated in: T. J. Kent, *The Urban General Plan* (San Francisco: Chandler Publishing Company, 1964).

it is clear that there is a broad range of possible planning agency organizational schemes. The debate over which scheme is best focuses on who the professional planners' primary client should be—the citizens' planning commission, the executive, or the city council?

Is There an "Ideal" Planning Organization?

The participants in the debate about planning agency organization usually make the implicit assumption that there is an "ideal" type of planning organization which agencies across the country ought to adopt. A close look at the evidence available casts doubt on the validity of this assumption. It is, therefore, likely that none of the debators will ever be declared the winner. Each of the debators has based his conclusions on very different perspectives concerning what planning and planners ought to be doing. Furthermore, quite different assumptions have been made about the nature of municipal government and communities. These different perspectives and assumptions are clearly not applicable to all planning agencies. For this reason the arguments used in the debate lack general applicability. The kinds of perspectives and assumptions are outlined below.[6]

1. The planners' objectives—provision of technical information versus the implementation of plans;
2. The scope of planning subject matter—technical physical considerations versus broader policy formulation;
3. The relative complexity of the issues with which the planner must deal and the extent to which these issues are interrelated with other municipal government activities;
4. The formal organization of municipal government itself.

Proponents of the Semi-Independent Planning Agency

One of the arguments in favor of the semi-independent planning agency is that the commission, composed of "respected" citizens in the

[6]Some of the perspectives and assumptions of the debate are discussed in greater detail elsewhere. See Frederic N. Cleaveland, "Organization and Administration of Local Planning Agencies," in Mary McLean, ed., *Local Planning Administration* (Chicago: International City Managers Association, 1959), pp. 40-75. Another discussion which stresses the differences in outlook between planners and professional administrators is also quite appropriate to the point being made here. Robert Daland, "Organization for Urban Planning: Some Barriers to Integration," *Journal of the American Institute of Planners,* No. 4 (1957), pp. 200-206.

community, will help gain acceptance for the planning function and lend prestige to the proposals of the professionals. The endorsement of the planning commission is also supposed to help gain favorable action from elected officials. This argument was originally made by the framers of the 1928 Standard City Planning Enabling Act.[7] This "endorsement" role of the commission was quite important in the early days of planning when the general public did not understand the need for public planning and many people felt it had a leftist ring to it. Today, planning still lacks acceptance in some municipalities, but in others the "endorsement" function of the planning commission is losing its value as planning becomes more and more accepted. Planning commissions will be most effective in municipalities with a relatively homogeneous population where the influence of an "elite" group of citizens may be considerable. Those who have used the "respected" citizens argument to support their position in favor of the planning commission have implicitly assumed that all communities have such an "elite" group of citizens. Yet there are many places where it would be extremely difficult to find a group of people to serve on a planning commission who would be respected by all elements in a community. In many large cities, for example, downtown businessmen, Negroes, and white ethnic groups have radically different ideas, goals, and perspectives relative to planning. In these cities it seems unlikely that all members of the planning commission could be equally respectable to everyone. Thus, while the influence of a citizens' planning commission may be great in some kinds of municipalities, that influence may be negligible in many other communities.

A second major argument in favor of the semi-independent planning commission is that planning should be free of "politics." The early proponents of this position were expressing a general distrust for municipal government which grew out of planning's reformist heritage. In addition, an assumption was made here about the scope of planning. Those who would equate politics and planning to drinking and driving assume a very narrow scope for the planning function. Planning is seen as a technical pursuit that has answers which can be phrased in terms of yes and no or right and wrong. Many planners today recognize that even such technical problems can involve differences of opinion which create a need for political settlement. Further, technical planning programs must compete with other municipal pursuits for money and attention. However, if one believes that planning should involve only questions of standards for the width

[7]U. S. Department of Commerce, *op. cit.*

of streets, the maximum density of the population, and similar matters, conflict is apt to be less and an independent status for the planning function may not be inappropriate. If, on the other hand, one stresses the need for planning implementation and takes a broader view of the scope of planning, the "no politics" argument makes no sense at all. Thus, those who would keep planning out of politics have generally viewed the objectives and scope of planning as the provision of highly technical advice. They have also tended to be very distrustful of their government.[8]

A closely related argument suggests that while planning cannot be separated from politics, there are differences between the kind of decision making that goes into planning and that which is involved in other kinds of municipal policy. Howard, for example, makes a distinction between activities which are amenable to "political" action and those which call for "civic" action.[9] Planning, he argues, is in the latter category. The objective of planning, according to Howard's view, is to "guide" private developmental decisions which cannot be regulated by the government. Such guidance is best achieved by "citizen leaders" rather than by persons who are seeking re-election. Clearly, Howard's argument is dependent on his perspective of the objectives and scope of planning. He does not place emphasis on implementation but rather on "guidance." Furthermore, he tends to limit the scope of planning to providing technical, and physical advice. To Howard there is little interrelationship between planning and other municipal activities. Finally, Howard's argument implies a lack of confidence in the ability of elected officials to do what the "citizen leader" can do. Howard's central thesis is that the acceptance or rejection of planning proposals by government does not depend on the organization of planning but on the attitude of the politicians. He feels that because of the nature of the planning function, the citizen planning commission can produce better technical results than elected officials. If a different set of assumptions about the nature of the planning function and of city government were made, Howard's argument would become less convincing. Under some circumstances (those assumed by Howard and others who agree with him) the semi-independent planning agency may be very appropriate. In com-

---

[8]An exception to this is Rexford Tugwell. He has been quite distrustful of government and has questioned their ability to handle the kinds of subject matter with which planners must deal. He sees the scope of planning, however, as being quite broad. Rexford G. Tugwell, "The Fourth Power," *Planning and Civic Comment* (April-June, 1939).

[9]John T. Howard, "In Defense of Planning Commissions," *Journal of the American Institute of Planners* (Spring, 1951), pp. 89-94.

munities where planning and city government do not fit the Howard assumptions, the story will be different.

Banfield and Tugwell have also argued for the planning commission on the grounds that planning is a different kind of function.[10] Unlike Howard, however, they argue that the scope of planning should be very broad. But similarly they doubt the ability of elected officials to engage in the kind of future thinking which they believe planning requires. Tugwell and Banfield believe the planner should engage in "developmental planning" which involves devising a picture of the city as it "ought to appear" in the future. Politicians, they argue, are concerned only with matters of immediate practical interest and thus the planner's role should be to expand the scope of realistic alternatives for the politician. In short, the semi-independent planning commission is justified on the grounds that planning is a function which is different from all others and cannot be handled by regular elected officials. Again this view may be applicable under the conditions which Tugwell and Banfield specify. Chief among these conditions is the assumption that the planning function should only be engaged in "developmental planning." Another assumption is that politicians will not accept or adopt policies based on futuristic thinking unless they are filtered through a group of "respectable" citizens. These conditions may be present under some circumstances but not under others.

Proponents of the Staff Agency

Those who feel that the planning function ought to be administered as an executive staff agency use two kinds of arguments. One consists of attacks on the planning commission and the other of positive statements regarding the logic of planning as an executive staff function. Robert A. Walker was an early opponent of the semi-independent planning commission.[11] In 1941, he visited 35 cities and concluded, as others have since, that planning was a failure. He attributed the weakness of the planning function mainly to the citizens' planning commission. Walker's assessment of the record of planning commissions was based on his view of what planning ought to be. He wrote that planning should be as broad as the scope of

---

[10]R. G. Tugwell and E. C. Banfield, "The Planning Function Reappraised," review of Robert A. Walker's "The Planning Function in Urban Government," *Journal of the American Institute of Planners* (Winter, 1951), pp. 46-49.

[11]Robert A. Walker, *The Planning Function in Urban Government*, (2nd ed.; Chicago: The University of Chicago Press, 1950).

municipal government, but that planning commissions were concerned almost entirely with zoning administration and similar narrow concerns. Those who disagreed with Walker often argued that his conclusions about the success of planning commissions were based upon an erroneous definition of success.

Walker also attacked planning commissions with the assertion that citizens who serve on them are unable to grasp the complexities of planning. This argument has been repeated by more recent foes of the semi-independent planning commission. One professional planner who recently served on a planning commission agrees with Walker. He told of a fellow commission member who boasted, "Last night I sat down for two hours and developed a master plan for our city. If the rest of you fellows would do the same, we'd really have a plan!" Other professional planners such as Edmund Bacon of Philadelphia, have argued that citizens' boards are quite competent and satisfactory.[12] Clearly, the competence of a commission to handle the issues which come before it depend on the backgrounds of members and the kinds of things the planning agency is doing. These conditions may vary and so will the relative competence of planning commissions.

A further argument leveled against the semi-independent planning commission is that the endorsement role of the commission is no longer needed. In addition, it is said that most commission members do not have the respect of the politicians. David Craig, for example, claims that planning is now accepted as a municipal function so the original requirement of a board of distinguished citizens to endorse planning is no longer needed.[13] Walker, among others, argues that commission members have little influence over politicians.[14] As suggested earlier, the validity of both of these arguments is based on the erroneous assumption that communities react to planning and planning commissions in a uniform way. It seems likely that the critics of the planning commission are correct in some communities but not in others.

---

[12]Edmund Bacon, "Comments on 'A Task Force Approach to Replace the Planning Board,'" *Journal of the American Institute of Planners* (February, 1964), pp. 25-26.

[13]David W. Craig, "A Plea for the Eventual Abolition of Planning Boards," *Planning 1963*, pp. 68-81. Nash and Durden agree to some extent as they note an evolution of planning administration which begins with informal action by community leaders and ends with complete integration with the city government and the developmental process. Peter H. Nash and Dennis Durden, "A Task-Force Approach to Replace the Planning Board," *Journal of the American Institute of Planners* (February, 1964), pp. 10-12.

[14]Walker, *op. cit.*, p. 164.

Positive arguments have been made by a host of planners and planning theorists in favor of the planning agency as a part of the municipal executive's (mayor or manager) staff. Practically without exception, proponents of planning as an executive staff agency view planning in very broad terms. They also see plan implementation as an important objective. Given the assumption that planning involves policy formulation as broad as the scope of municipal government, the planning function is supposed to be thoroughly integrated with that government. Furthermore, the implementation of plans and planning policy should involve the closest possible working relationship between planners and municipal decision makers. Henry Fagin, for example, has advocated the creation of a planning office which would be in charge of developing the physical master plan, budgeting, and coordinating all municipal governmental activities. This office, according to Fagin, would have to be in the executive branch of municipal government.[15] The need for the integration of the planning function with the rest of the government becomes greater as the scope of planning increases. If the planner is concerned with the implementation of his plans and if his planning commission is lacking in influence, closer ties with the municipal government would be desirable. However, if the planning function has a more limited scope, and if the members of the planning commission are politically powerful, arguments for an executive staff agency are less persuasive.

Those who have argued that the planning agency should be on the staff of the municipal legislature have also made a number of special assumptions. T. J. Kent, for example, bases his position on his experience in Berkeley, California.[16] The Berkeley planners accept Kent's concept of the "general plan." This dictates that developmental decisions should be based upon a broad set of policy statements concerning the future physical development of the city. The plan is to be a policy guide to decision makers. It has no specific proposals but provides only "inspirational" assistance. City council is the policy making body and the city manager serves as an advisor to the council and an executor of the council's policy. The planner reports directly to council but is also subject to a citizens' planning commission which, in Berkeley, appears to have very knowledgeable members. Thus Kent, who is quite satisfied with the way things are going in his community, has concluded that their organization for the planning function is the

---

[15]Henry Fagin, "Organizing and Carrying Out Planning Activities Within Urban Government," *Journal of the American Institute of Planners* (August, 1959), pp. 109-115.

[16]T. J. Kent, *op. cit.*

best. His conclusion is based on a specific perspective on the nature of planning and the implicit assumption that city council is the prime initiator of policy in all cities.

Some Generalizations About Planning Agency Organization

It should now be clear why there will probably never be an answer to the question of which planning agency organization is best. The debate on this issue has been based on such a variety of different assumptions that one could conceive of instances where all the debators might be correct. A useful approach to the question of planning agency organization would be to analyze the experience of a large number of different kinds of planning agencies. Comparative studies of this sort, however, are lacking. The Walker study of 35 planning agencies was one of the few efforts to go beyond an individual's experience with a few agencies.

One recent attempt to do a comparative study of the effect of planning institutions on the planning function is a survey conducted by Rabinovitz and Pottinger.[17] A questionnaire was distributed to planning directors and 201 responses were received. Seventy-seven of the respondents were directors of agencies responsible to the chief executive, 76 were responsible to an independent commission, and 48 headed agencies which had combinations of both types. On the basis of the opinions expressed by the planning directors, the authors could not find important differences among different types of agencies relative to the kind of planning being done, or the political involvement of the planner and the likelihood of plan implementation. There was some evidence that the members of the planning commissions had little prestige. Neither did they have the time or inclination to put forth the effort planning directors felt was needed. The authors concluded that many people have overestimated the ability of the planning agency organization to enhance the effectiveness of the planning function. They also suggested that the question of the most appropriate planning agency organization has been greatly oversimplified. It has failed to take into account the wide variety of municipal characteristics which could influence planning outcomes.

In spite of the fact that no single type of planning agency organization is best under all circumstances, it is instructive to examine the

---

[17]Francine F. Rabinovitz and J. Stanley Pottinger, "Organization for Local Planning: The Attitudes of Directors," *Journal of the American Institute of Planners* (January, 1967), pp. 27-32.

trends in city planning agency organization. These trends are presented in the table below.

TABLE 1*

APPOINTMENT OF FULL TIME PLANNING DIRECTORS 1948-63 CITIES OVER 10,000

	1948	1959	1963
Per Cent Appointed by Planning Commission	50.3%	26.2%	16.4%
Per Cent Appointed by Executive (Mayor or Manager)	36.7	54.3	62.0
Per Cent Appointed by City Council	8.0	14.3	10.1
Per Cent Appointed by Other Authority	2.0	4.6	6.3
Per Cent Not Reporting	3.0	0.6	5.2
Total	100.0%	100.0%	100.0%
	(163)	(302)	(427)

*Source: For the years 1948 and 1959, data was adapted from a table found in Frederic N. Cleaveland, "Organization and Administration of Urban Planning," *op. cit.*, p. 55. 1963 data was taken directly from the *Municipal Year Book of 1963.*

Of the full time planning directors serving cities with populations of 10,000 or more, the percentage appointed by an independent planning commission has been declining steadily. In 1948, the percentage was 50.3 per cent; by 1963 it had dropped to 16.4 per cent. Appointment by the executive, on the other hand, is becoming increasingly more popular. In 1948 only 36.7 per cent of the planning directors were appointed by the executive. By 1963 this proportion had nearly doubled. Thus, the trend in planning organization is to make the planning agency responsible to the executive. This does not mean that planning commissions are being abolished. Indeed, for the most part, they are not. It does mean, however, that in an increasing proportion of cities the commission is losing its position as the primary client of the professional planner.

Conclusion

There is no way of resolving the debate over which kind of planning organization is best. The answer to this question depends on a large number of assumptions and conditions which vary tremendously. The lack of comparative studies of different types of planning agencies makes it difficult to predict what the effect of a given kind of institutional arrangement will be on the planning function under a specified set of conditions. The most glaring error made by the participants in the planning organization debate was their implicit assumption that a given set of perspectives on planning and local conditions could be generalized to apply to all planning agencies. The scant evidence available indicates that such generalization is neither possible nor desirable. Too much emphasis must not be placed on the importance of planning institutions without considering other variables. We cannot conclude from this analysis, however, that the organization of the planning agency is an unimportant aspect of planning's governmental context. The formal lines of communication between the planner and the decision makers do have an impact on the way planning decisions are made. This is true even though that impact is not the same for all planning agencies. Because of a lack of research, we cannot say exactly how these formal institutional arrangements affect planning policy under different conditions. Further, we are not able to determine how important these arrangements are relative to other aspects of the governmental context of planning. Neither can we say how important the governmental context of planning is relative to the planner's heritage, and the management of conflict. For the present, the student and practitioner of planning must evaluate planning agency organizations on an individual basis. However, they must be aware of the issues that have been raised concerning the impact of planning institutions on planning policy formulation.

Intergovernmental Relations and Local Planning 4

There is much more to the governmental context of the planning function than the administrative structure of public planning at the local level. The planner at this level must work within a context of law, policy and financial assistance which comes from the state and Federal governments. Such intergovernmental relationships have become so complex that it is no longer fashionable for students of government to speak of "levels" of government in the sense that each separate "level" operates independently of the others. Interdependence now characterizes our Federal system of government. At one time students of American government referred to our Federal system as a "layer cake" where each level of government had its own duties and functions. Morton Grodzins used a more appropriate cake analogy by calling the American governmental system a "marble cake."[1] Henry Fagin, who apparently feels that the system cannot be described as a cake of any sort, has used the term kaleidoscope.[2] Whatever analogy is used, it is a fact that the administration and financing of local govern-

---

[1]Morton Grodzins, "The Federal System" in President's Commission on National Goals, *Goals for Americans* (Prentice-Hall, Inc., 1960), p. 265.

[2]Henry Fagin, "The Evolving Philosophy of Urban Planning," in Leo F. Schnore and Henry Fagin, eds., *Urban Research and Policy Planning* (Beverly Hills, California: Sage Publications, Inc., 1967), p. 316.

ment services are significantly affected by the policies of the state and Federal governments. Since the local planning agency is a part of the local government, the interrelationships between local, state, and Federal governments are a very important aspect of planning's governmental context. The present chapter will focus on those intergovernmental relationships that have the most significant impact on local planning policy.[3] Two kinds of relationships will be explored: states and local governments, and the Federal and local governments.

Local Planning and State Government

"Dillon's rule" that local government is a creature of the state suggests that local governments have no powers or authority beyond what their state governments give them. The powers and authority of local governments in different states may be quite dissimilar. In fact, it is important to note that local governments operate in a specific state-local governmental system which has been developed by the state. More specifically, local governments possess a particular mixture of administrative and fiscal responsibilities assigned them by statute and constitution. In addition, the state plays a regulatory role over the local governments' performance of these responsibilities. There are two ways in which the state-local system can affect the planning function. One is through the state's control over the kinds of services local governments provide and the other is the amount of money available to pay for these services. Such control affects the planner's work indirectly. Public services are a part of the environment for which the planner is responsible. The state's fiscal controls may also affect the funds available for the planning function. The state-local governmental system also directly influences the planning function by administrative regulations and, to some extent, by offering technical assistance.

States have a variety of fiscal controls over local governments. Most states have statutory and/or constitutional limitations on the amount of taxation local governments may levy and on the amount of money they are allowed to borrow. In addition, states specify the sources of revenue that are available to their local governments. Since local

---

[3]For an excellent text on intergovernmental relations, see W. Brook Graves, *American Intergovernmental Relations* (New York: Charles Scribner's Sons, 1964). A number of excellent studies of specific aspects of intergovernmental relations have been produced and published by the Advisory Commission on Intergovernmental Relations, Washington, D.C., U.S. Government Printing Office.

governments rarely have enough money to pay for all of the services they need, state financial assistance is another means of state control over local finances. State law also affects the amount of money local governments spend by determining which services they must provide. The welfare function, for example, is provided by local governments in some states and by the state government in others. A recent study has concluded that local governments' taxing and expenditure responsibility (determined by the state) is a key factor in explaining the general level of public activity in local governments.[4] In other words, the state's fiscal role is very important to the over-all operation of local government.

States exert a variety of administrative controls over their local governments. Governmental organization, the methods of selecting specified officials, and regulations concerning the formation of new governments are generally prescribed by the state. The rights of governments to consolidate, annex territory and incorporate are subject to state control. Direct controls over the administration of specific functions are held by all states. Education is probably subject to the most stringent administrative controls. Standards for the qualification of teachers and other personnel, and curriculum and textbook selection are often determined by state departments of education. The states have similar, although less extensive, administrative powers over a number of other local governmental functions.

Politicians and some students of American government have argued that states should not have such extensive control over local government. Thus, an alternative to the "creature" theory of local government known as "home rule" is in effect in many communities.[5] Without home rule municipalities must get permission from the state legislature for every possible change in procedure including personnel regulations, salaries and administrative organization. Local governments which have been granted home rule powers have more freedom in these and other areas. The precise meaning of home rule, however, is blurred by variations in its application from state to state. In some states, home rule communities are granted self determination only in matters involving routine housekeeping decisions. In other

---

[4]Alan K. Campbell and Seymour Sacks, *Metropolitan America: Fiscal Patterns and Governmental Systems* (New York: The Free Press of Glencoe, Inc., 1967).

[5]Many of the important arguments for and against home rule are summarized by W. Brook Graves, *op. cit.* Also see Lyle E. Schaller, "Home Rule—A Critical Appraisal," *Political Science Quarterly* (September, 1961), pp. 402-415. For a general discussion of the concept, history and application of home rule see, Charles R. Adrian, *Governing Urban America* (2nd ed.; New York: McGraw-Hill Book Company, Inc., 1961), pp. 180-188.

states home rule powers are much broader and involve zoning, building codes, land use planning and any variety of other kinds of policy matters which are primarily local concerns. The extension of home rule to specific communities also varies from state to state. A number of states have granted some home rule powers to certain classes of local government through their constitutions. Others have applied home rule only to specific communities. The theory behind home rule is that individuals create the state government for their individual benefit and, therefore, the actions of the local government should be determined locally. The need for greater fiscal flexibility and the ability to organize local government to meet specific local needs are among the major arguments for home rule. Some opponents of home rule have stated that the cry for more autonomy for local government ignores the fact that in metropolitan areas local governments are highly interdependent. Thus, greater centralization of authority rather than independence is needed. Many states have extended some home rule powers to their local governments. But even in these cases most of the initiative for local government administration still rests with the state.

Urban Government and State Government

One reason for some of the demands for home rule is that state governments have not been meeting the growing needs of local governments in urban areas. States have historically favored rural interests in their legislatures. This was quite appropriate when the United States was a rural nation. As urbanization and metropolitanism shifted the nation's population from the farm to the city and suburb, however, the patterns of representation in state legislatures remained the same. Some state constitutions, until recently, have based representation on geographical areas regardless of the distribution of population. Others have had apportionment formulae which give the more populous communities relatively less representation.[6] In 1962 the Supreme Court ruled in the case of *Baker v. Carr* that state representation must be related to the distribution of population in order to satisfy the "equal protection of the laws" guaranteed by the United States Constitution. Since that time many states have begun the politically explosive process of complying with court rulings which

---

[6]Gordon E. Baker, *Rural Versus Urban Political Power* (New York: Random House, 1955), p. 11. Baker includes a comprehensive discussion of the whole issue of legislative apportionment.

have followed from the *Baker v. Carr* case.[7] It is not possible at this point to predict what the impact of the reapportionment of state legislatures will be.[8] Some have suggested it will result in a coalition of rural and suburban legislators which will keep the big cities at a disadvantage. Others have argued that a more equitable system of representation will be the result. One thing is clear. The pattern of policies resulting from the heritage of rural dominance of state legislatures will not be completely wiped out in a few legislative sessions.

Rural domination of the state government has resulted in a distinct lack of state legislation aimed at benefiting urban areas. The rural communities have definitely received the most benefit from state fiscal policies. Formulae for state grants-in-aid and the choice of functions to be aided by the state have favored rural dwellers. In 1962, state aid to metropolitan areas per person was $7.47 less than the aid in non-metropolitan areas.[9] The administrative controls which states have over their local governments do not reflect any conscious effort to deal with those local problems which are peculiarly urban. A few states have created special agencies to deal with urban affairs, but their impact thus far has been minimal.

States and the Planning Function

Given the rural bias of state legislatures, it is hardly surprising that the states have not been very attentive to the planning of urban areas. Some states have created state planning agencies which are mainly concerned with the development of the state as a whole, however, these agencies have not been extensively involved with planning at the local level. Nearly all of the states' technical involvement with local urban planning agencies has been stimulated by the Federal government. Federal planning grants are funneled through the state to the local governments. This Federal requirement has caused many

[7]The *Baker v. Carr* case stimulated a series of suits by citizens to force their states to reapportion their legislatures. On June 15, 1964 the Supreme Court spelled out in detail the "one man, one vote," concept by a series of rulings on the apportionment of six states. These cases have become collectively known as *Reynolds v. Sims*. An excellent discussion of these cases and the entire apportionment question may be found in: *Representation and Apportionment* (Washington: Congressional Quarterly Service, 1966).

[8]This subject is discussed from the planner's point of view by: Peter H. Nash and Richard L. Strecker, "Legislative Reapportionment, Urban Planning and the Supreme Court," *Journal of the American Institute of Planners* (August, 1962), pp. 145-155.

[9]Campbell and Sacks, *op. cit.*

states to supervise the local agency's use of Federal funds. At times this supervision is coupled with some technical assistance.

States have their greatest impact on local planning through their planning statutes. Enabling statutes must be enacted before a local government can legally plan. These specify a variety of administrative requirements that must be met by all local planning agencies. All states have passed laws that enable certain classes of local government to plan. Generalization about the nature of these statutes is difficult because they differ considerably in detail. Fortunately, summaries of state statutes pertaining to planning agencies have recently been compiled[10] thus making generalizations about the nature of planning statutory law feasible.

In the previous chapter we noted that the organization of planning agencies is determined by the state government and that the determination of this organization has been greatly influenced by a "model" planning enabling act published by the U.S. Department of Commerce in 1928. A "model" local zoning ordinance was also published by the Department of Commerce at the same time. These "model" ordinances are still the basis for most state-enabling statutes. The fact that planning enabling laws, designed to meet the planning needs of 1928, are still in effect is an indication of the lack of state concern with the planning of urban communities.

State planning enabling statutes tend to be very comprehensive and detailed in their administrative control over local planning agencies. One area of control involves the distribution of planning powers among various classes of local governments. In all states there are laws which specify the kinds of local governments that are allowed to plan, enact and enforce zoning ordinances, and regulate subdivision development. All of the states allow municipalities to plan and/or zone and in most states counties are allowed to plan. Counties, however, do not control the zoning of incorporated areas.

Most states have rules about the general organization and composition of the local planning agency. Thirty-seven states specify that the planning function must be governed by an appointed and semi-autonomous commission or board. In 38 states there are precise statutes which specify the method of selecting the officials of the planning agency. Many of these statutes also specify the length of the planning commissioners' terms of office and the steps which must be taken in order to remove them from office. A number of states have

[10]Robert M. Anderson and Bruce B. Roswig, *Planning, Zoning and Subdivision: A Summary of Statutory Law in the 50 States* (Albany, New York: New York State Federation of Official Planning Organizations, 1966).

laws which set forth the duties of the planning agency. Such statutes sometimes include things which the agency *must* do, as well as those things which they *may* do. Twenty states, for example, require municipalities to adopt a plan. In 48 states there is some provision to allow for regional or metropolitan planning. These provisions vary from permission to form special regional planning agencies to legislation enabling several municipalities or counties to join together for cooperative planning efforts. In some cases regional planning is permitted *de facto* because the states have given planning powers to the counties.

The planning agency itself may or may not be charged with the responsibility for the administration of planning's major implementative tools—zoning and subdivision control. In a majority of the states, the planning agency is given this authority. Statutes relating to zoning and subdivision controls tend to be highly detailed. Most states require that both zoning and subdivision regulations serve purposes specified in the statutes. In addition they spell out the procedures which must be followed for the enactment, amendment, and appeal of both the zoning ordinance and subdivision regulations. In some cases the actual content and form of these local ordinances are specified. Finally, a number of states have special statutes which directly control specific kinds of land uses thus superseding any local zoning ordinance. Religious facilities, for example, may be exempted from strict compliance with a local zoning ordinance.

In general, the state enabling statutes control the outward organization and administration of the local planning agency. In some cases they limit the kinds of activities the local agency may perform. There are problems with such comprehensive state laws. The conclusion of the previous chapter that no single type of planning agency organization is equally appropriate for all communities, would suggest a need for agency structures which are tailor-made for individual situations. Specific statutes outlining the duties and general operation of the agency do not permit such flexibility. A further problem is the fact that most state statutes still reflect "model" ordinances written in 1928. The statutes themselves are a clear indication that the states have given little thought to the question of the appropriateness of their laws for the needs of today's urban communities. Perhaps as state legislatures are reapportioned this situation will change. At the present time, however, the role of the states in local urban planning is not very helpful. Part of the states' role is negative because rural areas are getting more benefits from the state governments than are the urban areas. The remaining involvement of the state in local planning has been almost entirely limited to the inflexible enabling laws and some technical assistance.

Local Planning and the Federal Government

Although the states have considerable legal control over the affairs of their local planning agencies, the impact of the states on local planning has been far less than that of the Federal government. The Federal government has played two roles in local planning activities. Indirect influence over planning practice and policy-making has been exerted through the establishment of Federal grant programs. These programs have been designed to help local governments cope with many problems which involve the planners. While a large number of programs have an indirect impact on planning, three types have been the most influential: housing, urban renewal, and transportation. The Federal government has also played a direct role in the planning of urban communities. Grant programs specifically designed to aid the planning function have been a great stimulus to city planning across the nation. Because these programs specify the kind of planning the Federal government will support, the Federal planning grants have a direct impact on planning practices.

The rationale for the involvement of the Federal government in local planning efforts has not been established overnight. It is partly the result of an evolution of thinking and subsequent program proposals by the President and his executive branch, and has partly developed from Congressional deliberation and debate over these proposals. The first Federal programs which had some impact on the planning of cities were established while planning itself was still in its infancy. These early programs were primarily a response to the great depression of the 1930's and were mainly concerned with strengthening a faltering market for housing. Gradually they were extended and expanded and the reasons for Federal involvement in urban planning became broader. Recently a subcommittee of the United States Senate has begun to take a long hard look at the rationale for the involvement of the Federal government in the cities. The assumptions behind this investigation as stated by the subcommittee chairman, Senator Abraham Ribicoff, are indicative of this rationale.

> For the crisis of our cities is the crisis of the modern United States. Seventy per cent of all Americans now live in or close to cities. The

number grows each year. So the fate of the city and the future of our country are one and the same thing.[11]

Thus, the current concern of the Federal government with the problems of cities has moved away from the original notion of simply bolstering the national economy. The Ribicoff hearings show considerable support for the idea that city problems are national problems. As we will see, the content of the current Federal programs in cities reflects the concept that city problems are indeed, national in scope.

The evolution of Federal attention to the problems of cities has proceeded on a program-by-program basis. Each program was designed to meet some specific need such as housing for the poor, declining business in the central city, and traffic problems. At one time or another, specific needs of our urban centers were perceived by the President and his executive branch or by members of Congress. If these needs were seen as national problems, legislation was initiated and programs were developed. In some instances the perception of needs in our cities came through the foresight of Federal government officials. More often it was stimulated by expressions of discontent from individual constituents or organized groups such as the United States Conference of Mayors or the AFL-CIO. Thus urban programs have been established without any declared national urban policy. In short, the Federal role in urban development has evolved through the *ad hoc* adoption of special programs designed to meet specific needs.

In spite of the lack of a clearly stated national urban policy, the sum total of urban programs has created a general undeclared policy of Federal support for cities. As Federal programs affecting cities multiplied, large groups of people have acquired a growing interest in the continuation of these programs. Cities have made commitments—political and economic—to remove slums, restore the downtown, and improve the flow of traffic. These commitments have been put on paper in the form of city plans and are based on the premise that Federal involvement in the cities will continue and grow. People who stand to benefit from these commitments have thus acquired interests in the Federal programs. For this reason the Federal government is now expected to use its financial and technical resources to make our

[11]Statement of Senator Ribicoff, *Federal Role in Urban Affairs*, Hearings before the Subcommittee on Executive Reorganization of the Committee on Government Operations, United States Senate, 89th Cong., 2nd sess., August 15 and 16, 1966, Part I, (Washington: United States Government Printing Office, 1966), p. 1.

urban areas better places in which to live. The tenor of the Ribicoff committee's inquiry is some evidence that the Federal lawmakers have accepted this policy. They are now looking carefully at their basket of urban programs to see whether all are moving in a consistent direction relevant to the needs of the urban municipalities.

Federal Programs and the Planning Function

Federal programs affecting the planning function, both directly and indirectly, have sometimes worked at cross purposes. Some programs, for example, have attempted to help cities recover from problems induced by the movement of people and industries to the suburbs. Other programs have encouraged this movement.[12] While inconsistencies in the results of Federal programs have cropped up from time to time, there have been some very clear trends with respect to the over-all impact of these programs on the planning function. These trends relate to the scope of planning being undertaken in cities (the subject matter of planning) and to the geographical area affected by local planning policy.

Those Federal programs affecting the scope of planning have tended to encourage broad planning activities, while the planning activity of local governments still focuses on physical development. However, Federal programs are using grants to encourage localities to enlarge this focus to include economic and social development as well. A second thrust of Federal planning programs has been to encourage the development of meaningful planning policies for entire metropolitan areas. Early aid to local planning agencies benefited only small individual municipalities. Recently, however, strong inducements have been offered to the municipalities within metropolitan areas to cooperate and develop coordinated planning policy on a metropolitan-wide basis.

The intent of the Federal programs has not, at this point, been reflected in local planning policy. Planning in metropolitan areas today is still largely physically oriented. Furthermore, the policies are geared to the goals of individual municipalities rather than to entire metropolitan areas. Nevertheless, the Federal planning programs have placed considerable pressure on local governments to change the thrust of their planning activities. Such pressures constitute a force which can influence the professional planner's initial recommendations for his community. It is conceivable that the Federal role in local

---

[12] Senator Robert F. Kennedy, *Federal Role in Urban Affairs*, *op. cit.*, p. 30.

planning could change the nature of planning policy in metropolitan areas. Thus, some knowledge of the evolution of those Federal programs which are apt to have the greatest influence on local planning is important. An understanding of the forces which have brought the Federal programs into being can significantly aid our understanding of the role the Federal government is presently playing in local planning activities. Some knowledge of the evolution of the Federal programs can also be useful for predicting the extent to which the Federal government is apt to change the planning policies and practices of local planning agencies in the future.

Increasing the Scope of Planning

The earliest Federal programs affecting local planning were designed to offset a disturbing rash of mortgage foreclosures during the great depression. Another aim of this same legislation was to stimulate home buying which had come to a standstill by the early 1930's.[13] During the 1920's the cities of our nation were growing and so was the market for homes. Big investors were speculating on land and small investors were buying houses. The year 1925 marked the peak of the home buying boom; 937,000 homes were purchased. The demand for mortgage credit became intense. Borrowers were overextending themselves and lenders found themselves with incredibly large holdings of low quality mortgages for both land and houses. As the American economy began its infamous descent in 1929, lenders began to foreclose on their mortgage holdings. During 1933, over 252,000 mortgages were foreclosed. The state of the mortgage market was only one dismal aspect of the depression. But Federal officials believed that by putting the mortgage market back in order, a significant step could be taken toward stabilization of the national economy. Thus, in 1932 the Federal Home Loan Bank Act was passed by Congress. This program provided loans to savings and loan associations to help reduce the pressure on the lenders and slow down foreclosures. In 1933 the Home Owners Loan Act was initiated enabling the Federal government to refinance loans when foreclosures were threatened. The Housing Act of 1934 had the greatest impact—both on the economy and the planning function. This act placed the credit of the United States between borrowers and lenders by underwriting the risk of mort-

---

[13]For a compilation of all Federal housing legislation between 1932 and 1965, see: Gilman G. Udell, *Home Owners' Loan Acts and Housing Acts* (Washington: United States Government Printing Office, 1966). An analytical treatment of Federal programs for urban areas between 1945 and 1965 has been put together by the Congressional Quarterly Service, *Housing a Nation* (Washington: Congressional Quarterly Service, 1966).

gages. The Federal Housing Authority (FHA) was created by the 1934 legislation in order to establish the conditions under which the Federal government would guarantee loan repayment. Among these conditions were lower interest rates and longer repayment periods than those offered by conventional mortgages. The FHA program has been extended over the years to the point that FHA mortgages now constitute about 15 per cent of the mortgage market.[14]

These early recovery measures were important to the planning function in two ways. In the first place, Federal involvement in the mortgage market has been partially responsible for the development of suburbs and the subsequent decline of the city by making it possible for city dwellers to buy homes outside of the city. These developments gave rise to a need for a planning policy that could control the growth of suburbs and fight off central city decline. Secondly, the early Federal housing legislation opened the door for the establishment of a Federal role in the development of urban areas.

In 1937 the adoption of a Federal public housing program opened this door even further. With the enactment of the Housing Act of 1937, the Federal government took a major step in their involvement with urban problems. In Section 1 of the Act it was stated:

> It is hereby declared to be the policy of the United States to promote the general welfare of the Nation by employing its funds and credit . . . to remedy the unsafe and unsanitary housing conditions and acute shortage of decent, safe and sanitary dwellings for families of low income . . . that are injurious to the health, safety and morals of the citizens of the Nation.[15]

Thus, slums were declared a national problem. In accord with this recognition, the United States Housing Authority was created and funds provided to establish public housing units throughout the nation. Under the public housing program, the Federal government paid for the construction of low income housing units and for a portion of the costs of the operation and maintenance of these units. The Federal subsidies were partially an anti-depression measure which kept rents sufficiently low so that poor people could have decent housing.

Throughout the 1940's the public housing program was continued, but it met increasing political opposition. The original critics of the

---

[14]For a good summary of the role of the Federal Government in housing see Glen H. Beyer, *Housing and Society* (New York: The MacMillan Company, 1965), pp. 448-483.

[15]U.S. Congress, Senate, Pub. L. 412, Chap. 896, 75th Cong., 1st sess., S. 1985, 1937.

program, organizations of home builders, real estate men, bankers, and the United States Chamber of Commerce, believing that public housing was socialistic, continued to fight it during every session of Congress. Efforts of President Truman and Democratic Congressmen to expand public housing were blocked. The only significant housing legislation enacted between 1938 and 1948 benefited World War II veterans. Many of the original supporters of public housing began to criticize the program when it became clear that, in spite of its efforts, slums were growing faster than the number of public housing units. In addition, the tenants were dissatisfied with the publicly owned and operated dwellings and showed their displeasure by breaking windows, and vandalizing.

By the end of the 1940's supporters of Federal housing legislation were asking for additional Federal effort. The central city was declining. The middle and upper income people were going to the suburbs, the city's tax base was shrinking, and slums were multiplying. These events caused groups such as the AFL-CIO, United States Conference of Mayors, National League of Cities, NAACP, League of Women Voters, and many others to support even greater Federal assistance to help the cities meet their problems. Such widespread group support for greater Federal aid to cities offset the opposition of the bankers, real estate industry, home builders, chambers of commerce, and other organizations who desired less Federal involvement in local affairs.

The victory for the proponents of a greater Federal role in urban affairs was manifested in the Housing Act of 1949. This act introduced the concept of subsidized redevelopment. Municipal governments could acquire slum property either by direct purchase or by eminent domain. In the case of eminent domain, private property could be condemned by local authorities and the owner would then have to sell it to the government for a fair price. Once the property was acquired, it was usually cleared and sold to a private developer who had to develop the land for a specific use determined by the municipal government. The price paid to the municipality by the developer was to be less than that which the municipality paid to the former owner of the property. The difference between the two sale prices was the amount of subsidy required to induce a private developer to develop land according to the specifications of local governmental officials. Two-thirds of the net cost of these transactions was paid by the Federal government.

The battle in both the Senate and the House of Representatives over the Housing Act of 1949 was intense. In fact, urban redevelopment had first been proposed in 1944 by Congressional committees in both the Senate and the House in response to national objectives outlined by President Roosevelt. Prior to 1949 opponents to the extension of the Federal role in urban affairs had been able to block urban redevelopment legislation. The rising pressures for Federal action generated by the mounting problems of urban communities apparently overcame the opposition. Sixty-four lobby organizations favored the 1949 legislation while only 25 such groups opposed it. In the Senate the act passed 57-13; in the House the vote was 227-186. In both cases, the Housing Act of 1949 passed easily.[16]

National policy toward the development and redevelopment of cities had been redefined by the 1949 legislation. Section 2 of the Act stated:

> The Congress hereby declares that the general welfare and security of the Nation and the health and living standards of its people require housing production and related community development sufficient to remedy the serious housing shortage, the elimination of substandard and other inadequate housing through the clearance of slums and blighted areas, and the realization as soon as feasible of the goal of a decent home and suitable living environment for every American family, thus contributing to the development and redevelopment of communities and to the advancement of the growth, wealth, and security of the Nation.[17]

This act had a significant, although indirect, effect on the planning function. The new Federal commitment to clear slums and strengthen the housing industry led to greater demands for planners who could assist in mapping out the physical details of urban redevelopment projects.

Between 1950 and 1953 very little legislation was passed that had any impact on urban areas. Controversy over public housing and redevelopment was still raging. In 1954 President Eisenhower introduced a comprehensive *omnibus* housing bill known as the Housing Act of 1954. The Eisenhower legislation had a rocky road through Congress. Much of the conflict over the 1954 Act centered on the public housing provisions. Conservatives criticized the public housing provisions for being too extensive and liberals criticized it for not being extensive enough. While the conservatives in the Republican controlled Congress were generally critical of the whole act, they focused their attack on public housing. As a result, appropriations for

---

[16]An important factor in this strong bi-partisan support was the leadership role played by Senator Taft.

[17]U.S. Congress, Senate, Pub. L. 171, 81st Cong., Ch. 338, 1st Sess., 1949, S. 1070.

the public housing program were significantly cut back. Furthermore, new public housing construction was limited to units needed to replace housing being torn down as a result of the redevelopment program. By concentrating their attack on the public housing program, however, the conservative elements let an important extension of the redevelopment program through almost untouched. The vote on the entire housing package was 59-21 in the Senate and 358-30 in the House.

The Housing Act of 1954 replaced urban redevelopment with the concept of urban renewal. This new concept was partly a response to criticism from proponents of housing legislation who claimed that urban redevelopment had resulted in an inhumane bulldozer approach to urban problems. The bulldozer approach had indiscriminantly eliminated the housing of the poor. Redevelopment projects had been adopted without careful analysis of the type of housing that should be eliminated. They were also adopted without the benefit of an over-all development plan, and without sufficient thought to the problem of relocating those people who would be displaced. Urban renewal broadened redevelopment to include assistance for the rehabilitation of existing structures which had deteriorated, and the conservation of buildings which were still in good shape. Furthermore, Federal assistance under urban renewal could not be obtained without prior approval of a workable program. A workable program consisted of proof that the execution of urban renewal projects would be consistent with Federal guidelines. These guidelines fell into seven categories.

1. The urban renewal project had to be based on a comprehensive plan;
2. The city had to have an ongoing building code enforcement program;
3. A blight analysis had to be made to determine which houses were to be eliminated;
4. The city had to have sufficient administrative machinery to carry out the program;
5. The city had to demonstrate an ability to pay its share of the cost;
6. The city had to make provisions for the relocation of all persons displaced by the project;
7. A program of citizen participation in the planning and execution of the project was required.

The Housing Act of 1954 also introduced the first direct assistance to the planning function. Grants were provided to state agencies for planning assistance to communities under 25,000 and to regional planning organizations. The grants were on a 50 per cent matching basis and were administered by the state or by an agency designated by the state. The type of planning to be funded was physical. Specifically the funds were available for "surveys, land use studies, urban renewal plans, technical services, and other planning work . . ." This provision has become known as the "701" planning grant. Its initial purpose was to "facilitate urban planning for smaller communities lacking adequate planning resources . . ."

The Housing Act of 1954 was a major extension of Federal involvement with urban problems. Consequently, it had a significant impact on planning. By enlarging and broadening urban redevelopment to include rehabilitation and conservation, the Federal government effectively created a greater demand for planners to help execute the new projects. The requirement of a comprehensive plan and certain studies as a prerequisite for urban renewal assistance, made the services of the professional planner even more in demand. Finally, the "701" planning grant was a boon to planning in many small developing suburbs. Again it should be noted that the kind of planning being stimulated by these programs was physical planning. The Federal involvement with urban problems up to and including the Housing Act of 1954 was primarily with the physical manifestations of these problems—housing, land use, community facilities, and public works.

In 1956, however, an extension of the urban renewal program marked the beginning of a new trend toward a broader Federal view of the kind of planning needed to properly execute urban renewal programs. The Housing Act of 1956 established the General Neighborhood Renewal Program (GNRP). This program provided grants for the establishment of renewal projects in "entire neighborhoods." These projects might be of different types—some requiring redevelopment, others rehabilitation, and still others conservation. Projects included in the GNRP were to be programmed over a ten-year period. Implicitly the GNRP required renewal agencies to think carefully about the different kinds of treatment needed in different sections of a community. It also required them to develop some criteria for establishing priorities among different proposed projects. These implicit requirements were a small but significant step toward a Federal policy to encourage the development of planning criteria that go beyond physical land use standards.

The Housing Act of 1959 went even further in this direction. The "701" planning grant program was amended to encourage comprehensive planning. The act spelled out in detail the elements of a comprehensive plan.

1. Preparation, as a guide for long-range development, of general physical plans with respect to the pattern and intensity of land use and the provision of public facilities, together with long-range fiscal plans for such development;
2. Programming of capital improvements based on a determination of relative urgency, together with definitive financing plans for the improvements to be constructed in the earlier years of the program;
3. Coordination of all related plans of the departments or subdivisions of the government concerned;
4. Intergovernmental coordination of all related planned activities among the State and local governmental agencies concerned; and,
5. Preparation of regulatory and administrative measures in support of the foregoing.[18]

The implication of points 2-5 was that the Federal government now saw the scope of planning as going beyond physical land use considerations. Planning now was to include fiscal programming and the coordination of all governmental activities affecting the development of the community.

This concept of comprehensive planning was also embodied in another portion of the 1959 act. Urban renewal was again expanded to include the community renewal program (CRP) to provide funds for a comprehensive study of the renewal needs of entire communities. Such a study would be aimed at producing a schedule or program of renewal projects for a whole municipality. The legislation stated that a minimum CRP should include an identification of blight and blighting influences; an assessment of the fiscal, economic, physical, social, and administrative resources available to meet renewal needs; and the development of a program of renewal action. The CRP was an extension of the thinking behind the GNRP. Community renewal programming required very broad based planning with analysis involving a total assessment of community development needs and developing criteria for establishing priorities among these needs. In speaking of the influence of the CRP on planning, one planner has suggested that:

---

[18]U.S. Congress, Senate, Pub. L. 86-372, 86th Cong., 1959, S. 2654, sec. 419.

> We planners are already borrowing the Cunard Line's snappy phrase, "Getting There is Half the Fun." For community renewal programming is diverting some attention from the final destination posed by the master plan or gleaming model and placing it instead on the critical path that leads from where a city is today to where it wants to be.[19]

The most recent and most important extension of Federal encouragement to broaden the scope of planning was the "Model Cities Program." This program was a part of the Housing Act of 1966. Generally, the program provided for Federal grants to cover 80 per cent of the cost of planning comprehensive development programs covering major sections of cities. If the planning phase of the program went well, there was a promise of further grants covering 80 per cent of the local share of other Federal programs that would be needed to implement the plans. The comprehensive attack on urban problems provided for in the Model Cities Program included the coordination of projects covering a broad array of different subject matter. The legislation has stipulated that projects should be designed to improve: (1) the general physical environment; (2) housing conditions; (3) transportation networks; (4) public education; (5) employment opportunities and economic development; (6) recreational and cultural facilities; (7) the reduction of crime; (8) health facilities; and (9) the quality of social services and public assistance.

The "Model Cities" legislation and guidelines further stipulated that a model cities agency must be set up in order to coordinate the programs and projects of all governments and agencies that would be involved with programs in the nine areas enumerated above. Benefit-cost and systems analysis were to be used in order to weigh the relative merits of various projects and project packages and to establish priorities and developmental programs. The "Model Cities Program" clearly encouraged a kind of planning that would concern itself with the entire physical, social, and economic fabric of the community, unlike the earlier Federal programs which only emphasized physical planning.

---

[19]Graham S. Finney, "CRP: The United States Experience," *Planning, 1965* (Chicago: American Society of Planning Officials, 1965), p. 194. For other commentaries on the nature of the influence of the CRP on planning see David A. Grossman, "The Community Renewal Program, Policy Development, Progress, and Problems," *Journal of the American Institute of Planners* (November, 1963), pp. 259-269; and Robert E. Mendelson, "What is the Community Renewal Program and What Can it Mean to East St. Louis?" (Edwardsville, Illinois: Public Administration and Metropolitan Affairs Program, September, 1966).

There is good reason to believe that the idea of encouraging broad-based comprehensive planning through Federal programs has wide support and acceptance at the present time. It is true that the "Model Cities" legislation had to overcome considerable opposition—particularly for its appropriations. This opposition was largely a manifestation of Republican efforts to cut domestic spending in general. In addition, some groups testified against the "Model Cities" bills on the grounds that they represented further "Federal intervention." This line of argument came from such organizations as the United States Chambers of Commerce, Mortgage Bankers Association of America, National Association of Real Estate Boards and the National Association of Manufacturers. Their positions on the "Model Cities Program" were similar to their positions on Federal housing and urban development legislation over the past twenty years. Interestingly enough, when the appropriations for "Model Cities" were threatened, *ad hoc* lobby coalitions composed of members of some of the opposition groups put on a strong campaign in support of funding the program. According to an analysis by *Congressional Quarterly Service*, strong lobby efforts by local civic and business groups who stood to benefit from "Model Cities," a group of twenty-one top business leaders, and an alliance of various individuals and lobby organizations called the Urban Coalition saved the "Model Cities" appropriations from complete annihilation.[20] The Urban Coalition included the Mortgage Bankers Association which had opposed "Model Cities" during Congressional hearings.[21] One must assume that many of the top business leaders and the local business interests who helped save "Model Cities" were also members of the Chamber of Commerce. This broad based lobby for "Model Cities" appropriations is some indication that the opposition to the program was largely part of a general effort of conservatives to impede President Johnson's "Great Society" program and to cut domestic spending. Support for the concept of planning which underlies "model cities" appeared to be widespread. The professional planners, mayors, labor, business groups, bankers, and many other groups supported the program. Such support is some

---

[20]"Pressures on Congress: Lobby Campaign Saves Model Cities Funds in House," *Congressional Quarterly* (June 9, 1967), pp. 979-984.

[21]In August, 1967, a formal meeting of the Urban Coalition was held to discuss objectives. Some of the statements from that meeting and a roster of participants has been published: *Emergency Convocation: The Urban Coalition* (Washington, August 24, 1967).

indication that future Federal programs will continue to encourage planning that is much broader in scope than traditional concern.[22]

Planning on a Metropolitan-Wide Basis

A second trend of Federal programs is an increasing effort to encourage the development of planning policy for entire metropolitan areas. Like the policy of promoting broad, comprehensive planning, Federal incentives for metropolitan planning have evolved gradually over a period of years. Many of the programs discussed above contained provisions relating to the geographic scope of the local planning function. Since these provisions were tied in with broader housing and urban development legislation, they were subject to the same political difficulties as the programs discussed earlier. Opposition to programs designed specifically to aid planning has been very sparse. In addition, there has been very little organized effort to block the concept of Federal encouragement of area-wide planning. There are however, considerable political difficulties in actually implementing planning proposals on an area-wide basis. These difficulties will be discussed in the following chapter. Interestingly enough, the opposition to the implementation of metropolitan-wide plans at the local level does not seem to have permeated the Federal level.

Early Federal programs in urban areas had no specific planning provisions. As noted above, the housing legislation of the 1930's and 1940's was largely concerned with building up the mortgage market, stimulating home buying and removing slums by providing public housing units. None of this legislation even mentioned planning. The Housing Act of 1949 financed urban redevelopment but planning was only implied. Furthermore, the 1949 Act was aimed almost entirely at the central city. The programs of grants specifically ear-marked for planning did not come into being until the enactment of the Housing Act of 1954.

The 1954 Act established the "701" planning grant. These grants were given to states who distributed them to eligible governmental institutions. Although grants could also be received by official planning agencies with the responsibility for regional and state planning, there is little evidence that the legislation reflected much effort to

---

[22]At the time of this writing a bill is before Congress which would broaden the definition of planning under the "701" Planning Assistance Grant to include human resource planning. Another bill would require 701 plans to be more closely related to over-all governmental decision-making.

encourage planning on a metropolitan-wide basis. In fact, the 1954 legislation fostered a marked increase of planning activity in individual municipalities. By strengthening planning in newly forming or recently formed suburbs, the original "701" program had the effect of encouraging highly fragmented planning policy within metropolitan areas.

In 1959, Section 701 of the Housing Act of 1954 was amended. Some of the changes in the "701" program were a clear indication that more thought was being given to the need for metropolitan-wide planning. The revised legislation stated:

> The administrator is authorized, in areas embracing several municipalities or other political subdivisions to encourage planning on a unified metropolitan basis and to provide technical assistance for such planning and the solution of problems relating thereto.[23]

Under the provisions of the 1959 Act, grants continued to be given to regional planning agencies, and the maximum size of the muncipalities receiving grants was increased to 50,000. To the list of the kinds of agencies eligible for "701" funds the following admonition was added.

> Planning assisted under this section shall, to the maximum extent feasible, cover entire urban areas having common or related urban development problems.[24]

The evolving Federal policy of encouraging metropolitan-wide planning was pursued even more vigorously in 1961. Section 701 of the Housing Act of 1954 was again amended. In the 1961 version, the intent of Congress to encourage planning for entire metropolitan areas was clearly spelled out. Furthermore, Congress expressed its consent for states to enter into interstate agreements in order to establish metropolitan planning across state lines. Additional funds were provided when planning covered "entire urban areas." The size of the Federal share of the "701 planning grant" was also increased from one-half to two-thirds.

In 1962 metropolitan planning agencies received another boost from the Federal government. Since 1956 the Federal government had been helping to build an interstate highway system. Funds were provided to state highway departments which would cover 90 per

---

[23]U.S. Congress, Senate, Pub. L. 86-372, 86th Cong., September 23, 1959, S. 2654, sec. 419(c).
[24]*Ibid.*

cent of the cost of highways included in this system. The Highway Act of 1962 inserted a new wrinkle in the highway program. The act stated that by 1965 all areas containing more than 50,000 people must produce an area-wide transportation plan in order to be eligible for the coveted Federal highway funds. This new requirement was responsible for much frantic activity in many metropolitan areas. These areas had intended to use Federal highway money, but there were few planning agencies that could produce the required plan. Thus, the 1962 Highway Act stimulated the formation of a number of metropolitan planning agencies.

In 1963, 1964, and 1965, further advancements in the direction of encouraging metropolitan-wide planning were made. Bills were introduced into Congress which would require a review of all proposed Federal projects by a metropolitan planning agency as a prerequisite for Federal funding. These bills were all defeated, but the seeds had been planted for legislation that could provide stronger Federal sanctions to promote metropolitan planning. In 1964, the "701" program was again amended in order to extend the emphasis on metropolitan-wide planning even further. The thrust of the 1964 version of the "701" program was to strengthen metropolitan planning agencies by offering them grants to undertake planning in individual municipalities within their jurisdictions.

The Housing Act of 1966 represented a very significant advance in the evolution of the policy to encourage metropolitan-wide planning. This act contained a proposal which was first introduced in 1963. It required review and comment from a metropolitan planning agency as a prerequisite for the funding of a large number of Federal grant and loan programs. Thirty-nine separate Federal programs were affected by this requirement. These programs originated from seven departments and two executive agencies. They covered projects for open space land acquisition, hospitals, airports, libraries, water supply and distribution facilities, waste treatment works, highways, transportation facilities, and water development-land conservation areas. In addition, the 1966 legislation proposed to make metropolitan-wide planning even more attractive by giving supplemental Federal grants for certain projects which had regional significance and were consistent with regional planning policy. The supplemental funds were to cover up to 20 per cent of the local share. Projects in the areas of transportation, water, sewers, recreation, open space, libraries, and hospitals were all potentially eligible for these supplemental Federal funds. The hand of the metropolitan planning agencies would be strengthened by the supplemental funds provision. It would give them an important role in the determination of local eligibility.

During the debate over the financing of these new laws, Congress backed down on their previous commitment. The supplemental funds for planning were cut out altogether. The House of Representatives stipulated that the Department of Housing and Urban Development could not use any of their funds or time to administer the provision of the Housing Act of 1966 that required review of certain kinds of Federal grant applications by a metropolitan planning agency. For this reason, the metropolitan planning agency review provision is, at the time of this writing, being handled by the Bureau of the Budget. It is clear, however, that there is a distinct trend toward greater Federal support for the concept of metropolitan planning. While early Federal planning grants promoted planning in individual municipalities, the emphasis of more recent programs has shifted. Although certain provisions of the Housing Act of 1966 were watered down by Congress, there does seem to be a general Federal attitude concerning the proper geographic scope of planning. The future manifestation of this attitude is likely to be the use of Federal programs to encourage planning on a metropolitan-wide basis and to strengthen metropolitan planning agencies.

Conclusion

In the present chapter we have been exploring certain intergovernmental relationships which are an important part of the governmental context of planning in metropolitan areas. Two kinds of relationships have been discussed: those between the state and local governments, and those between the Federal and local governments. The states have not paid too much attention to the planning done by their local governments. The historical rural bias of the state legislatures may partially explain the state's lack of concern with local planning. States through their constitutions and statutes have considerable legal leverage over the operations of local planning agencies. In most states the legislation governing these agencies dates back to the 1928 "Model Planning Enabling Act." The states' planning enabling statutes which were largely based on the "model" tend to be very detailed and inhibit local flexibility in the administration of the planning function. The Federal government has had much more influence over local planning policy than the state governments. This influence has evolved out of a series of urban programs involving grants-in-aid. Most of these grants have gone directly to the local governments. While there is no clearly defined national urban policy, the Federal programs do seem to be moving toward certain discernable objectives. The thrust of those Federal programs which influence planning the most has been to encourage planning which is broad in scope and which covers entire metropolitan areas.

Planning policy formulation is greatly affected by these intergovernmental relationships. The formal lines of communication and authority between the planning agency and the rest of the local government are greatly influenced by state government. As noted in the previous chapter, these formal relationships do affect the manner in which decisions about planning policy are made. The Federal government has used grants to influence local planning policy. The planner, whose services are largely financed by the Federal government, cannot overlook the intent of those programs which are his bread and butter.

Metropolitanism and the Planning Function 5

Much planning policy at the local level is formulated for the benefit of individual municipal jurisdictions which lie within metropolitan areas. These areas contain large numbers of governmental units which are physically and economically interdependent but politically independent. Planning policy formulated for the benefit of a particular municipality may actually be harmful to other parts of the metropolis. Because that policy was formulated by an independent political jurisdiction, however, aggrieved parties usually have little, if any, recourse. The planner must accommodate the goals of the political jurisdiction which has hired him. Thus, in order to understand how planning policy is formulated, we must understand how the development of metropolitan areas has produced interdependent municipal jurisdictions with basically different and often conflicting planning objectives.

The nature of metropolitan areas is a key aspect of the governmental context of the planning function. Initially we define what metropolitan areas are and explain how they have developed. Furthermore, the social, economic and political characteristics of the governmental jurisdictions within metropolitan areas are described. Given this background information, an evaluation is made of the influence of metropolitanization on the formulation of planning policy within metropolitan areas.

Metropolitanism and Urbanism

The birth of planning as a function of American local government occurred during the final years of the 19th century, when the problems facing cities were those associated with rapid urbanization. This process of urbanization was quite different from the more modern urban process which we call metropolitanization. A careful distinction between urbanization and metropolitanization is basic to an understanding of how the latter process is affecting the planning function today.

Urbanization involves a population concentration resulting from two forces. One of these forces can be described as rural push. Important changes in the technology of agriculture began in the early 1800's. Improved soil technology and the development of farm machinery made possible significant increases in agricultural productivity. In essence, farm land was beginning to produce more crops with fewer farmers. Between 1820 and 1840 the proportion of the labor force employed in agriculture began a continuing sharp decline. By 1880 less than half of the labor force in the United States was employed in agriculture. Farmers displaced by improved farm technology were forced to seek employment elsewhere. In a sense, they were pushed from the farm. Consequently, farmers who were victims of this rural push looked to the city for alternative employment opportunities.

About the time that the rural push was gaining momentum, industrial technology was changing. Mass production was becoming a feasible method of manufacturing a wide variety of goods. Firms began to specialize in the production of certain products. A decline in transportation costs opened wider markets for the goods being produced by the new industrial technology. For these reasons industries found it advantageous to concentrate in urban centers. These industries depended upon one another for goods, services, or materials that went into their final products. The developing economies of industrial concentration created increased employment opportunities in the nation's cities. Thus, changes in industrial technology established an urban pull which brought people from rural to urban areas. Employment opportunities offered in the cities made it the natural settling place for many immigrants who were coming to the United States at the turn of the century. Thus the rural push and the urban pull brought about a great migration of people to cities.

The relative concentration of the United States populace in urban areas during the 19th and 20th centuries is illustrated on the table below.[1] In 1800 only 6.1 per cent of the population resided in urban areas. By the turn of the century, this figure had risen to 39.7 per cent. By 1965 it was approximately 70.0 per cent.

TABLE 2

Percentage of United States Population in Urban Areas, 1800-1965

Year	Per Cent Urban
1800	6.1%
1850	15.3
1880	28.0
1900	39.7
1920	51.2
1940	56.5
1950	59.6
1960	63.1
1965 (estimate)	70.0

Source: U. S. Bureau of the Census, *1960 Census of Population, Volume I, Characteristics of the Population, Part I, United States Summary,* Table 3.

While an increasing proportion of the population is living in urban areas, the distribution of population within these areas has undergone a change. This has resulted in the formation of metropolitan areas.[2] Since the termination of World War II, a significant number of central city residents and industries have been moving out of the city, and settling in the surrounding area. The decentralization of population and economic activity within metropolitan areas is what we call

[1]The census definition of urban areas is used here. Basically the census defines any incorporated municipality with a population of 2,500 or greater as urban. Densely populated, unincorporated places are also included. U. S. Bureau of Census, *1960 Census of Population,* Volume I, Part I, pp. XXVI-XXVIII.

[2]There are two terms used in the discussion below which need definitions: "Metropolitan Areas" and "Central City." The Bureau of Census defines its Standard Metropolitan Statistical Area (SMSA) as an area containing at least one city or contiguous cities with a population of 50,000 or greater. Also included in the area is the county surrounding the city(s) and any contiguous counties which are "metropolitan in character." The city(s) with the population of 50,000 or more are the "central cities." The term "metropolitan character" involves the type of employment and density of population. For the complete definition see *U. S. Bureau of Census, op. cit.,* pp. XXXI-XXXII.

metropolitanization. It is a very different process from urbanization. Metropolitanization involves a spreading of people and jobs from the city outward. The fact that there has been a redistribution of people from the central city to the surrounding area is well documented by Table 3. Between 1900 and 1920 the proportion of the metropolitan

TABLE 3

Percentage of United States Metropolitan Population In Central Cities, 1900-1965

Year	Per Cent of Metropolitan Population in Central City
1900	62.2%
1910	64.6
1920	66.0
1930	64.6
1940	62.7
1950	58.7
1960	51.4
1965 (estimate)	48.0

Source: U. S. Bureau of Census, *U. S. Census of Population: 1960. Selected Area Reports. Standard Metropolitan Statistical Areas.*

population residing in the central city increased from 62.2 per cent to 66.0 per cent. During this period much of the non-central city portions of metropolitan areas were being used for farming. Since 1920 the situation has changed. The proportion of the metropolitan population living in the central city has been steadily declining. The greatest decline occurred between 1950 and 1960 when the proportion of central city residents fell from 58.7 per cent to 51.4 per cent. Thus, the process of urbanization resulted in a concentration of the nation's population in large cities. The more recent phenomenon, known as metropolitanization, has been characterized by people moving out of these central cities into the surrounding area or suburbs.

Just as there are a number of substantive reasons for urbanization, there are also explanations for the movement of people from the city to the suburbs. In fact, the forces associated with population decentralization are analogous to the rural push and the urban pull which underpinned urbanization. In the case of metropolitanization there was a city push and a suburban pull. The city problems brought about by rapid urbanization were fostering a considerable anti-city feeling among many of the city's residents. Noise, dirt, congestion, crime, the growing presence of slums, and a growing concentration of Negroes became forces which pushed those who could afford it to move out of the city. There were a number of economic and technological conditions that made it possible for people to satisfy their anti-city feelings and move out. In the post World War II period real incomes were rising. Secondly, home ownership became easier after the Federal government went into the business of guaranteeing mortgages. The Federal Housing Administration (FHA) entered the mortgage market during the depression and expanded its operations greatly after World War II. Another factor which facilitated the move to the suburbs was the growing ownership of automobiles and the subsequent development of highways connecting city and suburb. People who previously had to live near their place of work were able to commute from suburban residences.

As the suburbs began to grow, another force was set in motion which reinforced the push from the city. Suburbs soon developed features which attracted city people. The earliest suburban residents were primarily the most wealthy people in the area. Thus moving out to the suburbs became a symbol of having achieved a high social and economic status. Another aspect of suburban living that pulled people from city to suburb was the desire to own a freestanding house with a yard. This desire could be satisfied in the suburbs where land for home building was available at a reasonable price. Furthermore, suburban schools began to enjoy a good reputation which encouraged people to move from the city where the schools were older and on the decline. Finally, the contrast between the large city and the relatively small town atmosphere of many suburbs enhanced the attractiveness of the suburb. Some students of metropolitanism have argued that suburbia represented grass roots' democracy and a feeling of community that people could not find in the big city.[3] The idea that smallness in city size is an ideal that many Americans value is consistent with a recent Gallup Poll which indicated that 77 per cent of Americans would prefer to live in a place other than a city. Twenty-eight per cent of the people interviewed said that they wanted to live in the suburbs; 31 per cent preferred a "small town."[4] Thus, the

---

[3]Robert C. Wood, *Suburbia: Its People and Their Politics* (Boston: Houghton Mifflin Company, 1958); William M. Dobriner, *Class in Suburbia* (Englewood Cliffs, New Jersey: Prentice-Hall, Inc., 1963).

[4]Gallup Poll, printed in *Syracuse Post Standard,* March 3, 1966.

suburb's image of relative smallness strengthened its power to attract population. In addition, the presence of open space was also attractive to many would-be suburban migrants.

One other point about the movement of people to the suburbs is that the people who were moving out of the city did not represent all elements of the population. Migration from city to suburb was a sorting out process which created suburban communities with relatively homogeneous populations of white middle and upper income families. The cities were left with a concentration of people who had the lowest incomes, the least education, and who were predominantly non-white.

The population movements associated with metropolitanism were fostered and reinforced by a series of economic movements. These movements were initiated by both push and pull forces. Many retail establishments followed the population to the suburbs since it was important to be near the customer. Furthermore, the suburbs had certain characterisitics that made the move possible. Land values were lower, and space was in abundance. These characteristics allowed retailers to provide convenient parking space for their customers. The development of highway networks facilitated the movement of both people and products which also helped make the suburban location possible for the retailer. As retail establishments began to locate in the suburbs, sales in the city slowed. The convenience of suburban shopping centers and available parking spaces appealed to the suburbanite. In a study of 22 metropolitan areas, retail sales between 1948 and 1958 grew much faster in the suburbs than in the city. In the cities' central business districts, sales grew 2.9 per cent; in the central city as a whole the growth was 44.7 per cent; and in the metropolitan area, sales increased 62.1 per cent. Between 1958 and 1963 this trend became even more pronounced. Sales in the central business district declined 7.6 per cent. Sales in the central city as a whole grew only 9.2 per cent and metropolitan area sales increased 23.8 per cent. In all cases sales were growing much faster in the suburbs than in the central city.[5]

Further evidence of the greater relative growth of suburban retail business is presented in a recent study.[6] This study indicates that between 1964 and 1965 suburbs could claim over half of the value of

---

[5]The metropolitan areas were Los Angeles, Philadelphia, Detroit, Houston, Cleveland, Washington, San Francisco, New Orleans, Pittsburgh, San Antonio, San Diego, Cincinnati, Columbus, Indianapolis, Phoenix, Louisville, Portland, Fort Worth, Toledo, Birmingham, Rochester, and Omaha. The data was taken from: U. S. Bureau of Census, *Census of Business*, 1958, 1963.

[6]Dorothy K. Newman, "The Decentralization of Jobs," *Monthly Labor Review* (May, 1967), pp. 7-13.

building permits issued for new retail establishments. Also the payroll employment in retail establishments between 1959 and 1965 has been growing faster in the suburbs than in the city. As sales began to level off in the city, the remaining retail establishments began to feel an economic push to move to greener pastures. The out-migration of retailers has been most pronounced in the largest metropolitan areas. It is reasonable to assume that retail decentralization will become even greater in the future as the process of metropolitanization continues.

As retailers moved out of the city, a similar movement occurred among wholesalers.[7] A basic principle behind the location of wholesale business is to find a spot from which products can be moved with the most ease and the least cost. This spot tends to be at the fringe of the most highly congested areas in the metropolis. For this reason, the size of a given metropolitan area tends to become an important factor in the location of wholesaling establishments. In the larger metropolitan areas this location tends to be in the suburbs or at the perimeter of the city.

Many manufacturers have also moved their facilities out of the city.[8] A major reason for the outward movement of industrial plants was the lack of space in the city for modern operations. Many manufacturing establishments felt the need for increased horizontal space required by mass production. The large expanses of land outside of the city and the relatively low price of this land made suburban locations attractive. Aside from these push and pull forces, certain demographic and technological changes made the move to the suburbs feasible. The movement of people to the suburbs meant that there was a sufficient labor pool. Similarly, much of the metropolitan labor pool now had automobiles and could get to work from a variety of places. Thus from the labor point of view, there was much less of a constraint on industrial location. A technological change that made suburban industrial locations more feasible was the increased use of trucks to move materials and products. Lower shipping costs by truck and the flexibility of this mode of transportation enabled many industries to locate away from waterways and railroad lines. All of these factors helped facilitate the manufacturers' movement from city to suburb.[9]

---

[7]Raymond Vernon, *The Changing Economic Function of the Central City* (New York: Committee on Economic Development, 1959).

[8]*Ibid.*

[9]Hoover and Vernon have enumerated these factors in their study of the New York area. Edgar M. Hoover and Raymond Vernon, *Anatomy of a Metropolis* (New York: Doubleday Anchor Book, 1962).

Not all kinds of manufacturing activity found it advantageous to move out. Industries requiring low-wage unskilled workers remained in the city to be near their source of labor. Industries that used the products of other manufacturers for their own products have continued to find a centralized location advantageous. The clothing industry, for example, uses buttons and zippers that are made in nearby establishments. Such industries are said to benefit from external economies. Another kind of firm that has tended to stay in the city is the small firm that does not need large horizontal space. Such firms can often share quarters with other small industries and use the facilities available in the city.[10]

While some kinds of industries still find the central city a good location, many more do not. In fact, there has been a decline in the central city with regard to the amount of manufacturing activity occurring there. Between 1929 and 1958 the value of goods manufactured in the central city as a percentage of all the goods produced in the metropolis has declined.[11] In a sample of 13 metropolitan areas, central cities produced 66.1 per cent of the total value of the products produced in those metropolitan areas in 1929. By 1947 the proportion had fallen to 60.8 per cent; by 1958 it was 48.9 per cent; and in 1963 it was 46.4 per cent. Furthermore, data on building permits issued and payroll employment for manufacturing establishments indicates that between 1954 and 1965 industries have increasingly been locating in the suburban portion of the metropolis.[12]

Some Characteristics of Metropolitan Areas

The trends described above are the major elements of metropolitanization. It should be stressed that metropolitanization is an ongoing process and that the trends which have been discussed are continuing. In order to assess the impact of these trends on planning, it is necessary to see how far the decentralization process has progressed. The distribution of people, economic activity, and political jurisdictions within metropolitan areas can greatly affect the nature of the planning issues which arise in different parts of the metropolis. Thus, a close look at some current selected social, economic, and political

---

[10]*Ibid.*

[11]Vernon, *op. cit.*, and U.S. Department of Commerce, Bureau of Census, *1958 Census of Manufactures* (Washington: U.S. Government Printing Office, 1961); U.S. Department of Commerce, Bureau of Census, *1963 Census of Manufactures* (Washington: U.S. Government Printing Office, 1966).

[12]Dorothy K. Newman, *op. cit.*

characteristics of metropolitan areas is a necessary step toward understanding the relationship between metropolitanism and the planning function.

As already noted, metropolitanization has involved a sorting of population according to ethnic traits and socio-economic status. Those people of the highest socio-economic status (loosely designated as upper and middle class) are predominantly suburban dwellers. For this reason the people at the bottom of the socio-economic ladder are highly concentrated in the central city. The following table compares central cities to suburbs with respect to three socio-economic characteristics: income, education, and race. The differences between city

TABLE 4

Selected Socio-Economic Characteristics of
Cities and Suburbs

Characteristic	Central City	Suburb
Median Family Income (1959)	$5,945	$7,114*
Percentage of Persons 25 Years or Older With 4 Years of High School or More (1960)	40.9%	50.9%*
% Non-White (1960)	17.8%	5.2%**
% Non-White (1966)	22.1%	5.8%**

*The definition of suburb used here is what the Census calls "urban fringe" or the urbanized area surrounding the central city.

**Suburb is defined here as that area which is within the Census' "Standard Metropolitan Statistical Area" but outside of the central city. Such an area includes some semi-urban and rural places which is not true of "urban fringe."

Source: U. S. Bureau of Census.

and suburb shown in this table illustrate the impact of metropolitanization on the population distribution within metropolitan areas. Central city residents tend to have a lower level of income and education than suburbanites. These differences in income and education are largely a reflection of the fact that the central city is increasingly becoming the home of minority groups (particularly Negroes) who tend to have less education, less income and higher levels of unemployment. The increase in the percentage of non-whites in central cities between 1960 and 1966 is clearly demonstrated by the table. In addition, the data indicate that the presence of non-whites in the suburbs is low and relatively stable. The average percentage of non-whites in all central cities undoubtedly understates the situation. For in a few large cities, it appears that Negroes will soon comprise a majority of the population. Projections of population by race have been made in a number of central cities for the year 1970.[13] These projections indicate that by 1970 ten cities will have a Negro population which will constitute more than 40 per cent of the total city population. In 23 other cities the percentage will be at least 30 per cent, and in another 13 cities the percentage of Negroes will range from 25 per cent to 29 per cent. The suburbs, on the other hand, will continue to maintain their white population and enjoy higher incomes and educational levels.

The movement of economic activity away from the city has resulted in some significant differences between city and suburb with respect to the location of jobs. An increasing proportion of jobs within the metropolis are to be found in the suburbs. Earlier we noted that the suburbs were gaining a large share of the value of building permits for nearly all kinds of non-residential buildings, and a share of total payroll employment for retail and industrial establishments. Between 1956 and 1965, 49 per cent of the value of all non-residential building permits issued went to the suburbs. Between 1959 and 1965 the growth of payroll employment in a sample of 12 central cities was 12 per cent. The growth in the suburbs of these cities, however, was 30 per cent.

Metropolitanization has also affected the structure of local government. In 1962 there were 212 metropolitan areas containing 18,442 governmental jurisdictions or an average of 87 governments per metropolis. The number of governments in metropolitan areas is growing. At one time the increase in governments was the result of the incorporation of new suburbs and school districts. Today the growth is due to the formation of special districts which are responsible for one or more governmental functions such as fire protection, water supply, street lighting, etc. Generally, local government in metropolitan areas is fragmented with many overlapping jurisdictions. Governmental units such as counties, cities, school districts, and special districts possess a variety of powers. In many instances a given resident must depend on each of these kinds of governments for the services which all local governments provide for his benefit. This means that the responsibility for local public services is divided

---

[13]The projections were made for the U. S. Congress by the Center for Research in Marketing and are reported in *Congressional Quarterly* (August 26, 1966), pp. 1860-1863.

among a variety of governmental jurisdictions operating independently of each of the others.

Fragmented governmental authority and the variety of social and economic characteristics possessed by different governmental jurisdictions lead to diverse problems being faced by the many political units which make up the metropolis. To the extent that the problems connected with the development of a community vary in different parts of the metropolis, the issues confronting the planner will also vary.

Metropolitan Problems and Planning Issues: The Central City

In the central city there are a number of social problems. These are connected with the fact that the cities have a concentration of people with low incomes, high unemployment, and a low level of education and skills. Many of these people are Negro and suffer from racial discrimination, higher rates of disease, and a host of other manifestations of poverty. Among the more serious problems for these low-income families is housing. Discrimination and a low supply of decent low-cost housing places many central-city residents in substandard dwellings.

A recent study has concluded that one of the most difficult problems in the metropolitan economy is that of matching the growing number of jobs in the suburbs with the labor force in the city.[14] According to this analysis, there are numerous unemployed city dwellers who have the necessary skills for jobs which are available in the suburbs. Because many of these people are low-income Negroes, they are unable to live in the suburbs. Furthermore, the cost of commuting from the city to the suburb, in terms of money and time, is beyond the reach of this segment of the labor force. Thus the decentralization of economic activity from the city to the suburb has created a problem for the central city poor.

An additional problem facing the central city is the financial condition of the city governments. Metropolitanism has left the city with a shrinking revenue base. Deteriorating homes and fleeing businesses do not produce much tax money. Complicating the revenue problem is the fact that the demand for governmental services in the city is growing. Concentrations of low income families and heavy use of city facilities by commuting suburbanites place constant pressure on the

---

[14]Dorothy K. Newman, *op. cit.*

city for public services both in terms of quality and quantity. The costs of police, fire, water, sewer, street maintenance and other public services provided by local government are much higher in the city than in the suburbs.[15] One implication of studies of the education of children from culturally deprived areas is that they come into the school at such a disadvantage that more effort is required to give them a proper education.[16] This places great pressures on central city school systems to make higher expenditures for education. Finally the demand for public services in cities is increased by the concentration of a dependent population which has a great need for social services. A variety of different welfare programs is greatly needed in cities. Aid from states to meet revenue needs for these public expenditure demands has not been forthcoming. A heritage of malapportioned state legislatures has been that cities receive less financial aid from the states than the suburbs.[17] Federal aid programs do not offset this disparity. Thus, the cities are facing a mounting fiscal crisis where the demands for local public services in cities are far greater than the ability of these cities to pay.

Another set of problems facing the city as a result of metropolitanism involves the downtown businessman. The forces which pushed many downtown businesses to the suburbs continue to plague those businessmen who have remained in the city. The relatively easy access of suburban commercial centers has put the downtown businessman at a disadvantage. Traffic congestion, lack of parking facilities, and the presence of slum properties around business establishments make shopping and other activities in the city relatively difficult for the suburbanite. Thus many central city businesses are suffering. The fact that considerable financial investments have gone into these business establishments causes the downtown businessman to desire to counteract the condition of metropolitanism which has contributed to his plight.

The problems which the city faces shape many of the issues confronting the central city planner. To the extent that these problems are associated with metropolitanism, we can say that many of the

---

[15]Alan K. Campbell and Seymour Sacks, *Metropolitan America: Fiscal Patterns and Governmental Systems* (New York: The Free Press of Glencoe, Inc., 1967); Alan K. Campbell and Philip Meranto, "The Metropolitan Education Dilemma: Matching Resources to Needs," *Urban Affairs Quarterly* (September, 1966), pp. 55-56.

[16]See, for example, Martin Deutsch, "The Disadvantaged Child and the Learning Process," in Harry Passow, ed., *Education in Depressed Areas* (New York: Teacher's College, Columbia University, 1963), pp. 163-179.

[17]Campbell and Sacks, *op. cit.*

planning issues in the city represent the impact of metropolitanism on the planning function. To the extent that the problems in cities are different than they are in suburbs, we can conclude that metropolitanism has also influenced the kind of planning being done in different parts of the metropolis.

One distinct planning issue which is primarily associated with central cities has been precipitated by the problems of the city's poor. A broad goal of most planning efforts is to develop a pleasant and well-ordered environment. Given such an objective, central city planners cannot ignore the problems of the poor. Since low-income Negroes are increasingly dominating the cities, there is a need for a multitude of programs aimed at uplifting their income, education, and employment opportunities. Further, the plight of the poor has generated a need for the provision of decent housing for a population which is largely residing in slums. Efforts to deal with the problem of housing the poor have triggered a number of other planning issues.

Planners are frequently called upon to evaluate the housing of low-income people. Some housing may be classified by the planner as slum or substandard. This process of determining what is and what is not a slum has become a key issue associated with the low-income housing problem. One reason why it has become an important issue is that low income families and elderly people tend to be quite fearful of being moved out of their homes and into some unknown environment. Some critics have argued that planners use arbitrary standards when they designate a neighborhood as a slum.[18] They say that in his zeal to rid the city of what he considers poor housing, the planner overlooks certain aspects of the physical and social community that are highly desirable from the residents' point of view. This criticism has often been exhibited in conflicts between the planners and neighborhood residents.

Many planners agree that the treatment of substandard housing will vary depending on the physical condition of that housing. There is in reality a continuum of housing conditions which would call for treatment ranging from code enforcement to redevelopment. Code enforcement has always been a sticky planning issue. In order to maintain privately owned low-income housing at a decent level, cities must enforce minimal standards for housing unit maintenance. The enforcement of these codes is not always rigorous since landlords are usually more politically potent than their tenants. Nevertheless, code

---

[18]Jane Jacobs, *The Death and Life of Great American Cities* (New York: Vintage Books, 1963); Herbert Gans, *The Urban Villagers* (New York: The Free Press of Glencoe, Inc., 1962).

enforcement has been a major avocation of tenants associations and civil rights groups.[19] As a result, it has become one of the planning issues associated with low-income housing.

Once the planner has recommended the demolition of certain low-income housing units, he is faced with the question of what to do with the people who occupy them. Relocation has been a difficult planning issue since the redevelopment of cities began. Long periods of time between the official announcement of demolition and the establishment of relocation procedures, has caused residents to panic and move to another area of the city. In many cases their new location is slated for demolition at a later time. Even when the resident is willing to let the city relocate him, there are difficulties in finding a suitable place for him to live. The quantity of housing for low income Negroes is limited because of the small amount of rent they can pay and because of housing discrimination. One alternative is public housing. However, this procedure has been criticized by some of its residents on the grounds that it does not satisfy the housing needs of the low-income city resident and because it reinforces segregated housing patterns. The issues connected with relocation are admittedly difficult ones.

Another planning issue in the central city involves decisions on how redeveloped land should be used once the slums have been removed. The shortage of low-cost housing has led low-income groups to demand that planners use the land for homes which they can afford. But there are other kinds of pressures on the planner. Aside from public housing, it is difficult to find the private developers who can produce suitable housing units at a rent that low-income families can afford. Low-cost housing technology is in a sad state and consequently the only way to provide housing for the poverty budget is through governmental subsidy. In addition, there are extensive pressures opposing both public housing or any other low-cost housing developments as potential land use alternatives. Neither the city government nor the businessmen are enthusiastic about low-cost housing projects. They often attempt to force the planner to consider some alternative to low-cost housing. City governments are constantly looking for a way out of their fiscal crises. Public housing pays the city no property taxes and it is this property tax which provides city revenues. Low income housing that is privately owned pays less taxes than other land uses. Furthermore low income residents generate considerable costs for

[19]Code enforcement can have another dimension too. It can be used as a threat to the people living in substandard housing when these people cannot afford to move to another location.

public services. Thus the city governments have tended to view slum removal as an opportunity to bring developments to the city that will generate greater tax revenues and produce lower public costs for service needs. Thus the luxury high-rise apartment becomes a more attractive use from the fiscal point of view than any form of low-income housing. Not only will high priced apartments pay high property taxes but they will also bring upper and middle income people back to live in the city and help boost the slumping economy. Cities have also favored large business establishments as a replacement for slum property for some of the same revenue-inspired reasons.

Businessmen are generally in agreement with the city on the reuse of slum property. In addition, the difficulty faced by businesses in the city gives rise to another planning issue. Cities can only undertake a limited number of renewal or redevelopment projects at one time. The question arises as to which projects should have the highest priority. The business community favors an emphasis on renewal projects that will remove some of their difficulties. Thus projects around and near the central business district which will help to relieve congestion, provide parking for customers and remove unsightly slums are of highest priority to business groups. Since these same projects are often the most productive fiscally, the city government will also tend to favor them. Low income people, on the other hand, would like to see planning policy geared more directly to their housing needs. The establishment of priorities among renewal schemes is another important planning issue.

Metropolitan Problems and Planning Issues: The Suburbs

It is difficult to generalize about suburbs, suburban problems, and suburban planning issues. There are vast differences among suburban municipalities. Scores of writers have demonstrated that there are industrial, balanced, and residential cities which are geographically suburbs. Additionally, there are different kinds of residential suburbs. One writer has noted that suburbanites will move from one suburb to another as they rise in social and economic status. Thus, some suburbs have been termed "first-move suburbs" and others "second-move suburbs," the latter having the highest status.[20] All of the municipalities within a given metropolitan area could be classified along a continuum. The central city with its characteristic socio-economic

[20]Philip Meranto and Judith Launer, "Second-Move Suburbs," *Maxwell Review* (March, 1966).

attributes and problems would be at one end of the continuum. At the other end would be the residential suburbs which contain a homogeneous population of middle- or upper-income people. In between would be a range of different kinds of communities. It is simple to find examples of communities which are "suburbs" geographically but which have "central city" characteristics. In the discussion to follow the term "suburbia" refers to those municipalities which are at the other end of the continuum from the central city. Actually, the majority of residential suburbs are near the "suburban" end of the continuum. Thus generalization about planning problems and issues in suburbia is a useful way to illustrate that different kinds of communities have different planning problems and issues.

The planning issues which are predominant in the suburbs are different from the major central city issues. The main problems associated with suburbia are generated by the desire of suburban residents to maintain the character of their community. As decentralization in the metropolis continues, forces are set in motion which push some suburbs toward the central city end of the city-suburb continuum. Industries and lower income groups are constantly pushing outward from the city. To many suburbanites, these pressures constitute a problem. Since they moved out of the city (or out of a suburb with city characteristics), suburbanites tend to view any threat to change their new community into one that resembles the city as a problem. Specifically, many suburbanites do not want Negroes or other low income groups to live in their community. They also wish to avoid the noise, dirt, and congestion which they associate with the central city.

A second set of suburban problems is similar to those faced by the city. Suburbs also feel a fiscal squeeze but for slightly different reasons than the city. Rapid population expansion in the newer suburbs has created a need for extensive capital investment in school buildings, streets, sewers, and water supply systems. Further, suburban residents often demand a high calibre of local public services, particularly in their schools. Many suburban parents have college ambitions for their children and place a high value on education. As a result, they demand a first rate school system, which costs money. At the same time they own their homes and pay property taxes directly. Generally they are not happy about the amount of taxes they pay and do everything possible to fight attempts to increase their tax bill. Thus a high demand for services and a lack of enthusiasm for taxes are major factors behind suburban fiscal problems.

The desire of many suburban residents to preserve the character of their community gives rise to a major kind of planning issue. While suburbanites tend to agree that their suburb should be preserved in some manner, they do not always agree on specific formulations of this general objective. Actually, there are two aspects of the preservation issue which must be considered. One involves the basic question of what kind of community is being preserved. Conflict may arise over the question of whether planning policy should attempt to restrict specific kinds of people and economic activity from the community. The other aspect involves the determination of how to apply a restrictive policy to different parts of the community. The major tool used by the planner to implement a preservation policy is zoning, since ordinances are used by suburbanites as a restrictive policy.[21] Such a requirement as large minimum lot size for houses, or minimum floor space requirements for housing, can control the income levels of people who move into a community. In a few states minimum floor space requirements for housing can be used for the same purpose. Some zoning ordinances have excluded certain land uses such as trailer parks, multi-family dwellings, and heavy industry in order to preserve the community.

Planning issues in the suburbs are often aimed at resolving fiscal problems. Many suburbs have been engaged in a fiscal zoning game with a major objective of planning policy being to attract land uses which will pay more in taxes than they cost in municipal services.[22] Many planners consider fiscal zoning a hindrance to the application of planning principles, however, they recognize that such considerations have become an important part of local planning policy.[23] These fiscal objectives are not always in agreement with a desire to preserve the character of the community. Nevertheless, promotion of light industrial complexes or administrative industrial campuses in the suburbs provide a compromise. Commercial establishments and luxury multi-family dwellings can also find favorable acceptance in many suburbs for obvious fiscal reasons.

---

[21]Richard F. Babcock, *The Zoning Game: Municipal Practices and Policies* (Madison: University of Wisconsin Press, 1966); James G. Coke and Charles S. Leibman, "Political Values and Population Density Controls," *Land Economics* (November, 1961), pp. 347-361; Oliver P. Williams, *et al.*, *Suburban Differences and Metropolitan Policies: A Philadelphia Story* (Philadelphia: University of Pennsylvania Press, 1965), pp. 193-207.

[22]Seymour Sacks and Alan K. Campbell, "The Fiscal Zoning Game," *Municipal Finance*, Vol. 35, No. 4 (1964), 140-149.

[23]See, for example, the discussion of zoning in the New York Metropolitan Region by the Regional Plan Association. Regional Plan Association, "Spread City: Projections of Development Trends and the Issues They Pose," Bulletin 100, September, 1962, pp. 3, 31. Babcock makes a similar point in more general terms, *op. cit.*

The suburban-based planner finds himself with a set of issues which are different from those faced by his colleague in the city, but which have no less potential for conflict. The objectives of preservation and fiscal productivity are not always consistent with one another, nor with the planner's own professional assessment of appropriate planning policy.

Metropolitanism and Metropolitan Planning

Not only has metropolitanism been a determinant of planning issues in different parts of the metropolis, but it has also created pressures for metropolitan-wide planning policy. It is clear that present planning policy in metropolitan areas is as fragmented as the structure of local government. Planning policy is formulated on a municipal basis. From a developmental point of view, the governmental units within a metropolitan area are only politically independent. Physically and economically they are highly interdependent. When zoning policy is used in some municipalities to exclude certain kinds of people and land uses, some other municipal units within the metropolis must absorb them. It is possible for a single political jurisdiction to attract an industry and zone its residential areas so that the workers in that industry will have to live somewhere else. Thus, the cost of providing services to low-income workers is exported to another political jurisdiction with a less restrictive zoning policy. The municipality which accepts the low-income workers will be dependent on the community housing the industrial establishment for the employment of its residents. Further the industrial development in question might be located at the municipal boundaries adjacent to a residential section of a neighboring municipality. In short, provincial planning policy may have repercussions beyond the political boundaries of the community which establishes that policy.

Aside from the interrelationships among local planning policies, there are certain kinds of developmental projects and problems that cannot be confined within the borders of a single municipality. The control of air pollution and highway and mass transit developments are examples of projects which have extensive impact far beyond the borders of a single municipality. The location of highways and mass transit lines has a considerable influence on the location of other kinds of land uses and consequently on the growth patterns within a metropolitan area. The movement of people within the metropolis on the highways and mass transit systems must involve a coordinated transportation policy. Another policy area which would benefit from a metropolitan-wide approach is economic development. Policy affecting the metropolitan economy is in need of a regional approach if economic growth in the entire metropolitan area is to be maximized. The fact that there is a growing problem of qualified central city workers being unable to get to suburban jobs is a case in point. Many economists have suggested that from the perspective of economic development the location of political boundaries is irrelevant.

From a developmental point of view, the combination of high interdependence among metropolitan communities and a high degree of political independence of individual municipalities has generated conflicts among municipalities. Competition for fiscal resources is intense. The desire of some Negroes to move out of their ghettoes and the equally strong desire of suburbanites to keep the Negroes out of their communities creates another kind of conflict. In addition, a number of court cases over the practice of municipalities zoning out low-income people and undesirable land uses is evidence that the problems of cities and the preservative planning policies of suburbs are not in harmony.[24] Other court cases demonstrate the existence of disputes between municipalities over incompatible land uses at their borders.[25]

Inconsistent planning policies and a provincial approach to certain kinds of planning projects and issues that require a metropolitan-wide approach are reinforced by the highly fragmented governmental structure in our metropolitan areas. This state of affairs has brought about a strong demand from many planners and students of urban affairs for metropolitan-wide planning. At the present time large numbers of metropolitan planning agencies are in existence. As of 1963 a survey indicated that 142 out of 212 metropolitan areas in the United States had some form of metropolitan planning activity under way.[26] If the new Federal requirements for metropolitan planning under the Housing Act of 1966 are rigorously enforced, almost all metropolitan areas will have some kind of metropolitan planning agency in the near future. State governments have been cooperative in allowing local governments in metropolitan areas to engage in

---

[24]David C. Ranney, "Regional Development and the Courts," *Syracuse Law Review* (Spring, 1965), pp. 600-612.

[25]*Ibid.*

[26]*National Survey of Metropolitan Planning*, prepared by the U. S. Housing and Home Finance Agency for the Subcommittee on Intergovernmental Relations of the Committee on Government Operations, United States Senate, December 16, 1963 (Washington: U. S. Government Printing Office, 1963).

area-wide planning efforts. As of 1966 all but two states had legislative provisions for regional planning bodies.[27] But in the majority of states the involvement of state government with metropolitan planning has been limited to enabling legislation.

Although there are a large number of metropolitan planning agencies, they have not been able to bring about a metropolitan planning policy which is followed by the governments comprising the metropolitan areas. Charles Haar and his associates made the following observation on the basis of careful analysis of what the existing metropolitan planning agencies were doing.

> While metropolitan planning has been of value in most of these areas, the present agencies generally have been severely handicapped by small and uncertain budgets, insufficient legal power to permit active participation in development decisions and lack of clear statutory direction. . . . Although metropolitan planning agencies may wish to perform functions keyed to managing regional development, neither their funds nor existing statutory prescriptions have encouraged many of them to depart from population studies, economic analyses, and residential, commercial, and industrial land use planning.[28]

From Haar's report it is clear that metropolitan planning has not been an effective force in shaping metropolitan planning policy.

There are a variety of reasons why effective metropolitan planning has not been forthcoming. Ironically the very forces which have created a demand for area-wide planning constrain its effectiveness. The local governments within the metropolis have different objectives. Hence a truly effective regional planning policy would somehow have to iron out the conflicts which arise because of inconsistent planning goals. The fiscal pressures which produce policies aimed at maximizing revenues and exporting the costs of land uses, the housing and physical location of low income groups (particularly Negroes), and the question of where to put those urban activities which generate congestion, dirt and noise, are among the most touchy and conflict-laden issues which beset efforts toward metropolitan planning. There

---

[27] *The Effectiveness of Metropolitan Planning*, prepared in cooperation with Subcommittee on Intergovernmental Relations of the Committee on Government Operations, United States Senate by The Joint Center for Urban Studies of the Massachusetts Institute of Technology and Harvard University, June 30, 1964 (Washington: U. S. Government Printing Office, 1964); Robert M. Anderson and Bruce B. Roswig, *Planning, Zoning, and Subdivisions: A Summary of Statutory Law in the 50 States* (Albany, New York: New York State Federation of Official Planning Organizations, 1966).

[28] *Ibid.*, pp. 1, 42.

is evidence that mayors will support metropolitan planning agencies only so long as these agencies do nothing which will interfere with the provincial planning policies which have been developed to benefit individual municipalities. The United States Conference of Mayors, for example, has opposed legislation which would require regional planning as a prerequisite for Federal grants. The testimony on a Senate bill proposing such a requirement by the executive director of that organization is illuminating.

> The United States Conference of Mayors has supported Federal planning grants to metropolitan areas .... It is quite another thing to insist that such an agency be established and that all public works of a city be passed on to the agency for their comments .... We do not believe that it is a proper function of the Federal Government to interfere with local planning processes. To encourage regional planning is quite a different thing from requiring regional planning.[29]

Aside from issues of conflict within metropolitan areas, a strong American belief in the virtues of localism can act as a constraint on metropolitan planning. Robert Wood has argued that the wide-spread belief in small government and small society has discouraged regional governmental institutions and has strengthened the fragmented structure of local government in metropolitan areas.[30] A recent Gallup Poll further substantiates the claim that many Americans prefer to live in small places.[31] Preferences for small places and small government have been brought to bear on discussions of metropolitan planning. In hearings on the same Senate bill referred to above, the following opinion was expressed by a representative of a New Jersey citizens' group:

> Local government closest to the people, the bulwark of American freedom, will automatically be eliminated by regional planning agencies, whose scope of power goes beyond government power, absorbing even those of the private sector .... The question is not whether there shall be planning but who shall do the planning. At the municipal level it

---

[29]Statement of John H. Gunther, Executive Director, United States Conference of Mayors, in a letter included in the Hearings before the Subcommittee on Intergovernmental Relations of the Committee on Government Operations, United States Senate, 88th Cong., 1st sess. (Pursuant to Senate Resolution 45, 88th Cong.), May 21, 22, and 23, 1963 (Washington: U. S. Government Printing Office, 1963), pp. 173-175.

[30]Robert C. Wood, "Republics in Miniature," in Thomas R. Dye and Brett W. Hawkins, *Politics in the Metropolis* (Columbus, Ohio: Charles E. Merrill Publishing Company, 1967), pp. 326-334.

[31]George C. Gallup, *op. cit.*

> is controlled by the citizens; at the county level, the people become less important; at the state or Federal level, people are totally unimportant and become masses of humanity to be shifted about or pushed together in clusters for the sake of planners playing God.[32]

Successful metropolitan planning must overcome provincial planning policy that is rooted in individual municipal goals and a preference for localism. For this reason an effective metropolitan planning agency needs to be tied to a potent political base. The base should be a government that is responsive to local needs and attitudes.[33] Such a base is difficult to find. Outside of a very few metropolitan areas there are no regional governments in the United States. Single counties cover some metropolitan areas but in time the boundaries of such areas will be pushed outward. Furthermore, county governments are weak structurally. Many of them have no executive head and have a multiplicity of elected administrative officials. In addition, there are very weak links between the county and its municipalities.

Thus a county or multi-county planning agency is really not tied to an effective political system. Some regional planning agencies are forming using the council of governments plan (COG). Under this arrangement the planning agency is not tied to any one political jurisdiction but rather is composed of a governing body consisting of representatives from each of the major governments included in the region. The former Twin Cities Metropolitan Planning Commission in the Minneapolis-St. Paul metropolitan area had an arrangement of this type. A new council of governments has been recently formed in the Twin Cities with wider authority. The East-West Gateway Coordinating Council in the St. Louis area is another example.[34] The major difficulty with the council of governments scheme is that its members still must ultimately answer to local constituencies who have very definite stakes in localism. In short, such a planning agency

---

[32]Statement prepared by Mrs. Joan Tierney of the Tri-State Conference on Community Problems, Ridgewood, New Jersey, for *Hearings before the Subcommittee on Intergovernmental Relations,* May 21, 22 and 23, *op. cit.,* pp. 171-173.

[33]The need for metropolitan planning to be tied to an ongoing political system is urged by Alan K. Campbell at the *Hearings* cited above. *Ibid.,* pp. 110-118.

[34]For a discussion of the formulation of the former Twin Cities agency see, Roscoe C. Martin, *Metropolis in Transition: Local Government Adaptation to Changing Urban Needs* (Washington: U. S. Government Printing Office, September, 1963), pp. 51-62. For a similar discussion of the East-West Gateway Coordinating Council, see Seymour Z. Mann, "Across the Wide Mississippi," in Rocco J. Tressolini and Richard T. Frost, eds., *Cases in American National Government and Politics* (Englewood Cliffs, New Jersey: Prentice-Hall, Inc., 1966), pp. 19-33.

can only make metropolitan-wide policy that does not interfere with local planning objectives. Martin has noted that regional councils are successful when the problems they solve are non-controversial, when their solutions are not damaging in any way to any member of the council, when the execution of a policy does not require implementation by any local governments, and when the action required costs little or nothing.[35] Unfortunately, these conditions are rarely present in the formulation of meaningful metropolitan-wide planning policy.

Thus, even with the stimulus of Federal programs, future metropolitan planning is likely to be minimal. This is not to say that research and a clear delineation of the metropolitan implications of local policies has not been and will not be useful. Indeed such activities as existing metropolitan planning agencies can undertake are very much needed. But in the absence of finding a means to deal with those constraints on metropolitan planning which have been enumerated, comprehensive metropolitan planning policy which can overcome the inconsistencies and inadequacies of provincial planning practices is not likely to be forthcoming.

Conclusion

Metropolitanism has greatly influenced planning at the local level. The planning taking place in metropolitan areas today is being shaped more by the metropolitan context than by any other single factor. The planner's heritage, municipal administrative arrangements, and intergovernmental programs all must adapt to the overriding presence of the metropolis. The present chapter has demonstrated what the metropolitan context means to the planning function. Because of the distribution of population and economic activity within metropolitan areas, different problems and planning issues present themselves in different parts of the metropolis. Secondly, metropolitanism has generated certain pressures for area-wide planning. But metropolitan planning has not been successful. Planning in the metropolis is as fragmented as the structure of governments in metropolitan areas. The planner working within a given jurisdiction tends to address himself primarily to the needs of that jurisdiction.

---

[35]Martin, *op. cit.*, pp. 49-50.

6 Conflict and the Planning Process: The Politics of Planning

The previous chapters have stressed the influence of the planner's heritage, the governmental context of planning and most importantly metropolitanism on the planning function. Traditional planning ideology would suggest that these variables alone are capable of explaining planning policy formulation. The planner is supposed to be endowed with technical competence that produces decisions which are rational and reflect the public interest. Such technical competence should set him apart from the dirty business of bargaining over selfish interests which was presumed to be the content of politics. Those elected officials possessing the legal authority to formulate public policy were supposed to accept their planners' pronouncements with a sigh of relief. If they did not, the planner simply concluded that the politician was more concerned with his own selfish ambitions than with the good of the city as a whole.

Much to the dismay of the proponents of the traditional ideology, recommendations of the planner have not always been accepted by the elected officials with such enthusiasm. Frequently the planner has been totally ignored, or at best rebuffed. Sayre and Kaufman have pointed out that the Planning Commission's activity in New York City has resulted in disappointment and frustration to both itself and its supporters. The political isolation of the commission has not worked in practice. With the exception of a few minor triumphs, its efforts have been continuously thwarted by the governmental officials who, it was thought, would accept their recommendations without question.[1] Gradually planners have begun to realize that any kind of public policy (planning included) affects individual values. Since all people within a governmental jurisdiction do not generally share identical values, public policy formulation will usually be accompanied by conflict. The process of resolving or managing conflict over public policy is what politics is all about.

In many ways the metropolitan environment described in the previous chapter shapes the nature of the politics of planning. The distribution of social and economic characteristics in metropolitan areas has created a situation where very different kinds of planning issues arise in different parts of the metropolis. This fact has two major political ramifications. In the first place it becomes very difficult to plan on an area-wide basis as was stressed in the previous chapter. Secondly, planners in different parts of a metropolis will confront very different kinds of politics. This point will be a major concern of the present chapter.

In order to illustrate how the politics of planning differs in different parts of the metropolis, it will be necessary to discuss politics and planning first in general terms. A number of political concepts are introduced which will be used as a basis for generalizing about the politics of planning in central cities and suburbs.

Planning, Values, and Conflict

There are no planning policy decisions which do not involve value judgments. Consequently the formulation of planning policy is often accompanied by conflict as Norton Long points out:

> The question is not whether planning will reflect politics, but whose politics will it reflect. What values and whose values will planners seek to implement?[2]

In the course of making recommendations based on technical considerations, the planner is also making value judgments. The alloca-

[1]Wallace S. Sayre and Herbert Kaufman, *Governing New York City* (New York: Russell Sage Foundation, 1960), pp. 372-380.

[2]Norton E. Long, "Planning and Politics in Urban Development," *Journal of the American Institute of Planners* (November, 1959), p. 168.

tion of land to particular uses in a city plan, for example, has both technical and value content. How much land should be devoted to housing for low-income families in a community and what priority should low-income housing have relative to other aspects of a city's physical development? Those low-income people who feel that their present living facilities are inadequate would favor a plan which places a very high priority on the development of housing units that meet their needs. The downtown merchants who feel that they need to have more affluent customers living nearby, would favor a plan which places a high priority on replacing "slums" with middle and upper-income housing or with parking garages. Whose values come first in this case, the low-income slum dweller or the downtown merchant? This is quite clearly a matter to be solved through the political process. While there are definitely technical considerations in this issue, there is also a need to weigh the values involved. In short, both professional planning service and political considerations must be the basis for much planning policy.

Whether he likes it or not the planner is a key participant in the politics of planning. His initial decisions will often generate actual or potential conflict. The planner may decide to alter his initial decisions in order to avoid conflict. Alternatively, he may go out and drum up support for his proposals from the community, or make his decisions in line with his own values and ignore the politicians.

Some elected official or groups of such officials must ultimately decide how or if they should act on the planner's recommendations. In some situations the mayor or city manager may have the responsibility for action on planning proposals while in other circumstances the council or a number of different officials will have this authority. On the assumption that elected officials wish to be reelected, it is likely that such officials will be very interested in the political implications of planning policy recommendations. The elected official will search for a policy that will produce the most satisfaction on the part of his constituency and the least dissatisfaction. Sometimes there will be a need to persuade the voters of benefits to be derived from a given policy. At other times the politician will have to compromise his or his planner's position in order to satisfy powerful and dissident groups.

Describing how planning recommendations are transformed into public policy through the political process is complicated. The relative amounts of technical and political content of a planning decision will vary from issue to issue and from community to community. Likewise the methods employed to manage or resolve conflict will vary. These variations are due to a large number of variables which determine political behavior relative to planning in a given community. Unfortunately, the politics of planning has received very little attention from students of political behavior. For this reason much of the discussion in this and the following chapter consists of a series of hypotheses based on general studies of local political behavior, case studies of planning decision making, and the personal observations and reasoning of the author.

Conflict and Political Involvement in Planning

The politics of planning, like any kind of politics, is dynamic. The issues which arise today and the resolution of these issues are greatly influenced by decisions which have been made in the past. Planning policy formulation thus involves a continuous series of interactions between the planner, governmental participants in the planning process and non-governmental participants. The flow diagram presented in Chapter 1 illustrates these interactions. Private groups or individuals react to proposed or actual planning policy by making demands on elected public officials or on the planner. The elected officials in turn make demands on the planner either as a result of pressure from private groups and individuals or in anticipation of that pressure. In addition, some governmental officials may become actively involved with a planning issue if they perceive that the outcome of that issue will affect their position in the government. The participation of governmental officials may take the form of direct pressure on the planner to alter his recommendations, specific action based on the planner's recommendations, a lack of action on these recommendations, or pressure on some other governmental official.

The extent of these interactions which we can label "political involvement" has a great influence on the degree of potential or actual conflict which a planning issue will generate. Thus a knowledge of the kinds of things which prompt groups and individuals to become involved with a planning issue is essential to an understanding of the politics of planning. In general, the scope of political involvement can be understood by determining why certain groups and individuals are apt to take political action on a given issue, uncovering the means which they have at their disposal to influence the resolution of the issue, and observing how they utilize their influence. Put in the language of the flow diagram developed in Chapter 1, the questions are as follows. Who are the actors? What are their stakes in the resolution of the issue in question? What political resources do they possess? How well do they use those resources?

A number of studies dealing with political involvement in local government have used the concepts of actors, stakes, and political resources to explain how decisions are made in the local political arena. The findings of some of these studies and the theoretical frameworks which they have employed, have been used as a basis for explaining the general nature of political involvement in planning policy matters.[3]

The actors in the politics of planning consist of governmental officials and employees as well as individuals and groups who do not work for the government. Some elected officials of the local government are automatically involved in the politics of planning since they must ultimately decide to act or not to act on the recommendations of the planner. In some municipal governments the chief executive (the mayor or city manager) will introduce planning legislation to the council or act directly on the planner's recommendations. He may also respond to actual or potential pressures from either non-governmental or governmental actors before a decision is made. In other municipalities the council members assume these duties. Aside from the elected officials, other governmental employees may decide to become involved in the resolution of a particular planning issue. Such involvement is most likely when an individual feels that the planner is dealing with a policy area in which his department or agency has an interest. In examining a conflict over the location of a major highway in St. Paul, for example, Alan Altshuler noted that the planners and the highway officials became major adversaries in the dispute.[4] Since many planning issues affect departments within the local public bureaucracy, local administrators are often actors in the politics of planning.

A number of the governmental actors in planning are not employed by the same government for which the planner works. Some of these public officials work for other local governments. As noted in the previous chapter, the impact of many municipal planning policies reaches far beyond the boundaries of the municipality making that

---

[3]Three studies have been relied upon for this purpose: Sayre and Kaufman, *op. cit.*, especially Chapters II, III and IV; Robert A. Dahl, *Who Governs? Democracy and Power in An American City* (New Haven: Yale University Press, 1961), especially Chapters IV and V; Roscoe C. Martin, Frank J. Munger, *et al.*, *Decisions in Syracuse* (Bloomington: University of Indiana Press, 1961), especially Chapter I.

[4]Alan Altshuler, *The City Planning Process: A Political Analysis* (Ithaca: Cornell University Press, 1966), Chapter I.

policy. When a local jurisdiction is affected by the planning policies of a near-by municipality, its governmental officials will generally try to influence such policies. Officials of state and federal governments frequently become involved in local planning decisions. The extensive role of the Federal government in local planning through the many Federally funded programs makes their participation in numerous local planning decisions almost automatic. Since in many states the state government assumes an oversight role in local planning, the state officials can become involved with local planning issues.

There are several kinds of non-governmental actors who often play a substantial role in the politics of planning. The electorate as a whole is at least indirectly involved. Elected officials who wish to be reelected will not adopt planning policies which they believe will be unsatisfactory to many voters. These officials would encourage policies that will yield tangible results in a short period of time. Large building projects, for example, show the electorate that their elected representatives are doing something. In this manner, the electorate is generally involved in the politics of planning. Depending on the planning issues at stake, a variety of private groups and individuals enter the process of planning policy formulation more directly. Local businessmen frequently become active participants in the resolution of planning issues. Real estate people will be involved in most decisions that affect the real estate market. Neighborhood associations, *ad hoc* citizen groups and private individuals will take an active stand on planning policy when it affects them personally. Labor organizations concerned with the welfare of their members sometimes speak out on planning matters. Finally the mass communications media will often push for the victory or defeat of various planning proposals.

All of these governmental and non-governmental groups and individuals do not concern themselves with all of the planner's recommendations. Instead groups and individuals are highly selective about the planning issues in which they become involved. Some knowledge of the kinds of things that motivate people and groups to take an active part in the resolution of specific planning issues aids in understanding political involvement and conflict generation. It is very difficult to accurately assess human motivation in specific situations, however. In general terms, people become politically involved in a planning question when they feel that they have a stake in the matter.

There are different kinds of stakes leading to political involvement. One is acquiring or maintaining an elected office; or related to this, the desire to advance politically. This kind of stake is particularly important for those elected officials who have the responsibility for acting on the planner's recommendations. Their reaction to his plans will be greatly affected by the possible political ramifications of any action they might take.

A second stake in the outcome of planning policy decisions is economic. Many individuals and businesses stand to gain or lose money and/or jobs as a result of the implementation of planning policy. Central city businessmen, for example, have economic stakes in the redevelopment of central business districts. In one large midwestern city, it was proposed that an extensive residential area be redeveloped as a commercial center which would effectively create a new central business district. Those businessmen whose establishments were located in an existing district fought the plan because they felt it would affect them adversely. They clearly had economic stakes in this planning issue. The redevelopers who planned to invest in the proposed development had favorable economic stakes in the issue, since if the plan were adopted they would make money through their investment.

A third stake in planning involves the level of services offered by the government. An example is the capital improvements program which schedules all of the municipality's capital investment. New fire stations, school buildings, and major street improvements are among the things covered by these programs. Clearly those individuals who place a high value on the quality of a school's physical plant would have a public service stake in the priorities established in the capital budget.

Stakes are not always as tangible as public office, jobs, money, and services. Involvement with the politics of planning can also be motivated by a desire for prestige, power, feelings of altruism and other intangibles. Sometimes an ideological belief such as an aversion to Federal government programs in local areas causes citizens to fight against urban renewal projects. Sayre and Kaufman have observed that the goal of having a master plan as a guide to local policy is itself an ideological stake for certain groups in New York City.[5] It is difficult to determine who might have intangible stakes, since the people who have such stakes cannot always say exactly why they have become involved in a conflict over a particular issue.

Many of the groups and individuals who become involved in the politics of planning have a combination of these different kinds of stakes. The extent of the combined stakes of particular groups or individuals in the outcome of a planning issue does not necessarily

---

[5]Sayre and Kaufman, *op. cit.*, p. 42.

determine the final decision. The political influence of the actors in the politics of planning may be very unequal. Influence over the decisions of the planner and the elected officials partly depends on the possession of political resources. Just as there are different kinds of stakes in planning policy, there are also different political resources which individuals or groups can use to influence public decisions. The vote is a very significant political resource. Those who can control a large number of votes find their viewpoints on planning policy very important to those elected officials who must ultimately make such policy. There are many other kinds of resources which determine the ability to influence voters and/or those who control votes. Money is one resource which can be used in many ways including bribery or the financing of political campaigns. Control of jobs is another important political resource with the promise of employment influencing the way people vote. Thus the person who can provide large numbers of jobs can be politically influential. Another important resource is control over information. Those who own the local newspapers and the radio and television stations have considerable potential political power since the news media can determine what kinds of information the public will receive. It is not unusual for contestants in a planning conflict who lack control over public information to publish and distribute information themselves. One's social standing or popularity can be a political resource since an individual who is well known and respected will generally be able to find a sympathic audience for his views on an issue. Technical knowledge is another resource in planning issues. The planner frequently uses his expertise as a source of power in resolving planning conflicts. While the position that "I know I'm right because I'm a professional planner" is far from infallible, there is evidence that it is convincing to some people when it is backed by a certain amount of technical know-how.[6] Closely related to such technical expertise is the resource of knowledge. The planner, for example, is in an excellent position to know what the future impact of alternative policy proposals is apt to be. He has at his disposal the results of a wide range of studies which his staff has made. Potentially this information can be used by the planner to influence the outcome of many issues which arise. Knowing how to get federal grants can also be a very important means of influence.

---

[6]Two writers have concluded after looking at a number of case studies of conflicts over urban renewal plans that technical knowledge is a very significant source of power for settling these kinds of disputes. Sheldon J. Plager and Joel F. Handler, "The Politics of Planning for Urban Redevelopment: Strategies in the Manipulation of Public Law," *Wisconsin Law Review* (Summer, 1966), pp. 724-775.

Cities in need of funds will listen closely to those with a proven ability to acquire money from outside sources. A further type of political resource is fear. Negro groups in the central city have sometimes utilized the threat of widespread violence as a means to influence planning policy. One final type of political resource is legality. Governmental officials all have a certain amount of legality on their side by virtue of the formal powers which they possess. The mayor in a strong mayor-council government has a considerable legal resource due to the importance of the kind of public decisions he can legally make. The city council members also have extensive legal resources.

A knowledge of the distribution of stakes and resources relative to a planning issue is not a sufficient basis for predicting the role that groups and individuals will play in deciding that issue. All groups and individuals do not utilize the resources they have in an equally effective manner because of differences in the extent to which persons and groups will use the resources they have and how efficiently they employ those which they use. Dahl has made a useful distinction between actual and potential influence.[7] No groups or individuals completely realize their potential influence unless they are fully utilizing all of the resources they have at their disposal. It is doubtful that there is ever a time when all of the people and groups with political resources are completely aware of their potential influence. Thus at any point in time there will always be potentially influential actors on hand who are not using all of their political resources. The stakes in the outcome of a planning issue will partially determine how much of the slack resources will be taken up. There are other more intangible factors which determine the use of resources such as a knowledge of how to use resources and the ability to see how political involvement will further one's goals.

Prediction of the political consequences of planning policy under these circumstances is not an easy task. The political analyst whether he is the planner, the politician or an academician will have great difficulty determining whose stakes will be involved in a given planning issue. The problem of slack resources complicates prediction even further. As Campbell has suggested, a land use pattern at any time is associated with an extensive assortment of vested interests. It is very difficult to tell how a change in this pattern will affect all of these interests.[8] The unused political resources in the system can

---

[7]Dahl, *op. cit.*, pp. 271-275.

[8]Alan K. Campbell, "A Political Science Approach to Planning Change," *Planning Socio-Economic Change* (Raleigh, North Carolina: Agricultural Policy Institute, October, 1964), pp. 57-69.

suddenly be used by their owners with dramatic and unforeseen consequences.

The concept of slack resources is useful in explaining the uncertainties in the politics of planning and in understanding the behavior of elected officials relative to planning issues. As an issue begins to take shape, the political decision makers will take note of who is involved and who is not involved. A knowledge of the many individuals and groups with stakes in an issue who are not using their resources can influence the elected officials' reaction to the planner's recommendation. A politician will be reluctant to commit himself to a planning policy if the political consequences of that commitment are highly uncertain. Since the distribution of the costs and benefits of planning policy are often difficult to determine, there is apt to be a somewhat negative political environment for the implementation of planning proposals. Even when costs and benefits are known, the potential opposition will often be stronger than the potential support. The benefits of planning are sometimes abstract and obscure or they are geared chiefly to future generations. The costs of implementing planning policy through a change in the physical, economic or social structure of the city are, on the other hand, direct and immediate. Thus, the likelihood that those bearing the costs of planning policy will organize for opposition is fairly great. The probability that the beneficiaries of planning policy will organize to support that policy is much lower. The existence of slack resources in the local political system will, therefore, cause the political office holder to look unfavorably at those planning proposals which he associates with potential conflict.

The Politics of Planning in Cities and Suburbs

The politics of planning takes different forms in different parts of the metropolis. Put another way, metropolitanism is a key variable in explaining the nature of the politics of planning. The discussion to follow will use the general political concepts presented above to illustrate this point. The previous chapter laid much of the groundwork for this discussion by looking at two extreme community types, the "city" and the "suburb," and noting the different kinds of planning issues which arise in each community. The discussion of the politics of planning to follow has used the same general framework as the previous chapter by looking at "cities" and "suburbs" separately. Since many of the planning issues in the "city" involve saving the downtown and the need for low-income housing, the problem of slum clearance and redevelopment has been utilized to demonstrate the nature of the politics of planning in the city. The slum clearance issue enables us to discuss the politics of some of the most common decision situations which the central city planner faces. Since many planning issues in the "suburbs" are concerned with the best way to preserve the community, our discussion of suburban planning will focus on the political ramifications of a change in the zoning ordinance. This often involves the choice between preserving the basic character of the community and gaining public funds. Therefore the zoning question is a very appropriate vehicle for discussing the politics of planning in the "suburbs."

Central City Planning: Slum Clearance and Redevelopment

The process of clearing slums and redeveloping the land raises some of the most difficult and conflict laden issues faced by the central city planner. In theory, when a municipality tears down buildings and replaces them with others, there should be a substantial planning effort involved. In practice this is not necessarily the case. The decision to redevelop a particular site may be based upon recommendations contained in a general city plan, or it may be made because a private redeveloper has expressed an interest in a particular site. Those city planners who work for the city planning agency may, in fact, not even be involved with redevelopment. In many cities, redevelopment is handled by a semi-autonomous authority or by a separate department within the city administration. In these cases, the agency which is responsible for redevelopment has its own planners who may or may not confer with the general city planners. For the purposes of the discussion to follow we will consider that individual who is formally responsible for slum clearance and redevelopment as "the planner." This avoids the complication of the variety of arrangements that exist between the city planners and the redevelopment planners. It should be pointed out, however, that conflict over redevelopment has developed between planners in different agencies.[9] To make the discussion manageable we are omitting this type of conflict.

A number of major questions are raised and answered in the course of a slum clearance and redevelopment project. Among these are:

---

[9]Struggles between the city planners and the Newark Housing Authority is described in: Harold Kaplan, *Urban Renewal Politics: Slum Clearance in Newark* (New York: Columbia University Press, 1963).

What is a slum? Among the slum areas in the city, which should be cleared first and why? What should be done about the people and businesses which are located in an area slated for clearance? What improvements shall be put in the area after it has been cleared? What inducements must be offered to bring about the kind of redevelopment which the city feels is appropriate? Quite clearly many groups and individuals have stakes in public policies which involve these questions.

Actors and Their Stakes

Many of the actors in the process of slum clearance and redevelopment are involved because their job requires it. We might say that these actors have "institutional stakes." Since most clearance and redevelopment projects are subsidized by the Federal government under the Urban Renewal Program, Federal administrators are automatically actors. The Urban Renewal Program requires planners to formulate a general plan for the city, handle the administrative duties connected with the project, and prepare the site plan. The mayor or manager and the council become actors when official participation of the local government is legally required for clearance and redevelopment projects. Developers who will purchase the land from the city and develop it also have institutional stakes. In addition, a variety of middlemen such as bankers, real estate brokers, and lawyers are needed to conduct the complex business side of clearance and redevelopment.

There will always be political interests at stake in a slum redevelopment project. A number of mayors have used such projects to gain further political support by providing the voters with concrete evidence that they are doing big things for the city. The story of Mayor Lee's success with the urban renewal program in New Haven has inspired many other mayors to attempt to make good politics out of slum eradication. Furthermore, an ongoing program of clearance and redevelopment brings with it a lucrative source of rewards for the loyal constituency. Demolition and building contracts, improved streets in strategic areas, and a plan that brings great economic benefit to key businessmen are examples of the potential sources of patronage which a project can provide for the politician. Individual politicians may find that a proposed project affects relationships with their constituents. A Negro councilman, for example, may discover that urban renewal will remove his Negro constituents and replace them with wealthy white apartment dwellers. Other councilmen may discover that their constituents have personal stakes in the council's decision, thus, their action on a redevelopment proposal will affect the number of votes they receive in the next election.

Personal prestige and power are also at stake when slum clearance and redevelopment occur. A clearance project may, for example, be an opportunity for indivduals within the local government to become more influential. In Newark, Kaplan's study demonstrated how the head of the Newark Housing Authority gained considerable prestige through his ability to control clearance and redevelopment projects.[10] Community leaders with a reputation of influence and power have sometimes found it necessary to try to block or change a renewal plan in order to preserve their reputations. Civil rights leaders have made issues out of projects proposing to displace Negroes as a means to preserve their reputation as successful fighters for Negro rights. Prominant businessmen have become involved in disputes over slum clearance because certain groups were looking to them for leadership. Individuals who have been informally designated as local neighborhood leaders, have taken up the cause of saving the neighborhood from urban renewal as a means of consolidating their position in that neighborhood.[11] Finally, politicians who become embroiled in a dispute over a proposed redevelopment project will find that their prestige and reputation are on the line.

Slum clearance and redevelopment also involve professional stakes. The many planners who become involved in setting up the details of a project have a professional stake in seeing to it that their ideas are reflected in the policy that is finally implemented. This stake is partly a matter of personal prestige, but in a wider context the professional principles of planning are at stake. Planners particularly are sensitive on the matter of professionalism because as a group they are still establishing themselves as a recognized profession.[12] At times the planners must engage in a competition with other groups who also feel that their professionalism is at stake. The advice of lawyers, engineers, planners and other groups are not always in accord. Bureaucrats in the Federal government also have professional stakes in Federal Urban Renewal projects and must see to it that projects which are Federally funded are successful. There may be a variety of other kinds of professional stakes involved in a given slum clearance and redevelopment project, but these are the major ones.

---

[10]*Ibid.*

[11]J. Clarence Davies III, *Neighborhood Groups and Urban Renewal* (New York: Columbia University Press, 1966), pp. 178-81.

[12]Altshuler, *op. cit.*, Chapter VIII, pp. 392-408.

Slum clearance and redevelopment projects will always affect the distribution of income and jobs in a community. Thus there are a variety of economic stakes that are generated by these projects. Direct economic benefits will go to private developers, the contractors who demolish old structures and build new ones, and the real estate people who own the site of the project. Middlemen such as bankers, lawyers and real estate brokers who are called upon to handle the business aspect of the project also enjoy economic gains. A number of indirect economic benefits will be generated by any successful clearance project. Businessmen in the vicinity of the project may get wealthier clientele, or more parking space for customers. Improved traffic flow resulting from the project can make certain business establishments more accessible. It is possible that city governments will enjoy increased tax revenues to ease their fiscal problems. If commercial facilities are located on the site, jobs may be generated. There are also direct economic costs that will accompany any project. The small businessman who is forced to relocate will lose his former customers and he may be unable to get new ones in his new location. The site resident who is forced to move is not always sufficiently compensated for his expenses, and he may find it necessary to pay more for comparable housing elsewhere.

There are also social stakes in redevelopment. Observers of the redevelopment process have discovered that many site residents become highly insulted when planners designate their neighborhood as a slum.[13] In addition, these people may have strong social ties to their present location which would be shattered if they were relocated in another area. Such people generally oppose the redevelopment of their neighborhood because of these social stakes. The voices of those with such stakes in redevelopment seem to be getting louder, creating an important force in the politics of redevelopment planning.

One further kind of stake which people may have in slum clearance and redevelopment is ideological. Most communities have a number of civic booster organizations which are dedicated to the objective of improving the city. These are often supported by the news media in their promotion of business, good government, and solutions to municipal problems. Since slum clearance and redevelopment projects are usually proposed as a step toward the improvement of the socio-economic well being of the city, the civic boosters and their supporters have ideological stakes in supporting them. Other groups may

---

[13]Herbert Gans, *The Urban Villagers* (New York: The Free Press of Glencoe, Inc., 1962); Jane Jacobs, *The Death and Life of Great American Cities* (New York: Vintage Books, 1963).

have an ideological stake in opposing projects. Right-wing organizations and individuals with conservative views will sometimes fight programs that are financed with funds from the Federal government. Many of these organizations and individuals feel that urban renewal is socialistic. In one community, for example, Federal Urban Renewal was labeled the "FUR Trap" and called a communist plot to confiscate private property! Thus the ideological stakes of the right-wing will often generate very vocal opposition to redevelopment when Federal money is involved. Similarly, "black power" organizations who adhere to the philosophy that practically any public program which imposes costs on the Negro community and reaps benefits for the "white power structure" should be opposed, will fight most slum clearance projects.

Thus the stakes in slum clearance and redevelopment are varied and the actors holding these stakes are a cross-section of any urban population. All of the actors do not have an equal ability to influence redevelopment planning policy since political resources are not evenly distributed, and vary considerably. It is possible, however, to make some generalizations about the distribution of resources.

Political Resources and Redevelopment

Planners tend to have several different resources such as technical skill and knowledge. The extent to which decision-makers will listen to the advice of planners is greatly influenced by the technical competence which the planners exhibit or are presumed to have. The special training and experience of the planner in the areas of the relationship among land uses, urban design, and the economic and social consequences of developmental policies qualify him as an expert.[14] Many planners also have a firm grasp of the technical ins and outs of the Federal grant program requirements. The complexity of these programs makes this knowledge a significant political resource in itself. Aside from this knowledge the planner also has a legal role in slum clearance and redevelopment which can be used as a resource. In Newark, for example, the city planning commission is the legal authority designated by the state to decide whether or not a given site is "blighted" and hence eligible to be declared an urban renewal project.[15] Other requirements for Federal funds such as a comprehensive plan and a site plan have also established a legal

---

[14]It has been argued by some critics of planning that the planners do not have as much of a technical basis for their proposals as they need. See, for example, Altshuler, *op. cit.*, Chapter V.

[15]Kaplan, *op. cit.*

political resource for the planner through which he may influence public policy.

Officials of the Federal government can also influence the character of a local slum clearance project by virtue of their legal position. In order for a city to qualify for Federal funds, the Department of Housing and Urban Development must be satisfied that the Federal regulations have been met. Federal officials can also use the money which they control as a political resource since this often makes the legal status of Federal officials meaningful.

City officials have a variety of political resources which can be used to influence redevelopment planning decisions. Certain members of the city administration have technical skills which are essential in the planning of a project. For instance, the city engineer and the public works director have knowledge about road capacities, sewage and water systems and other developmental hardware. The city attorney's skills are needed at many steps in the redevelopment process including eminant domain proceedings, negotiations with potential developers and in handling the many contractual agreements which redevelopment generates. The mayor or city manager is a key figure in slum clearance decisions in most municipalities. Among the resources of municipal executives are the prestige of office, the knowledge of how to conduct the city's complex business, the staff of experts who work for him, political skills, the ability to be a clearinghouse for all information which flows into city hall and access to patronage such as jobs, information, contracts, etc. The city councilmen have similar political resources in most cities. Where a strong-mayor form of government is operative, the mayor is apt to possess the most formidable resources. In a council-manager government the city councilmen will be the most powerful elected officials.

Non-governmental actors also have resources which make them very important participants in clearance and redevelopment policy making. The private developer has access to the money and credit needed to redevelop the proposed site. Naturally he will not invest his money unless he is certain that he will get a sufficient profit. His ability to make the investment will thus become the means by which he influences the nature of the plan. The middlemen (lawyers, bankers, and real estate brokers) who are needed to complete all of the negotiations have skills which are a political resource.

Big businessmen who feel that a proposed project will affect their business interests or prestige have considerable means to influence the decisions made in city hall. For one thing they have money as a resource which can be used to pay city taxes and finance political campaigns. Often big businessmen also enjoy a good reputation and a high social standing in the city. Therefore, their views are respected by many voters and politicians. In addition, the businessman provides employment for many city residents which gives him support from the community.

Civic booster groups have political strength partly by virtue of the ideological stance they represent. It is difficult to oppose such ideals as improving the city, more jobs, better living conditions, and a government which works for the "public interest." The membership of the civic booster groups often includes the big businessmen and various other economic and social notables in the community who have resources of their own. The news media generally support the causes of the civic booster which gives him an important information resource. Thus the newspapers often favor redevelopment since much of their advertising comes from the downtown businessman. Obviously the "power of the press" is considerable when they control most of the public information about a clearance project.

The site resident generally has few political resources as an individual. His potential influence lies in the ability to organize. Davies found in his study of neighborhood groups in New York that it was easier to mobilize groups against a project than for it. Furthermore, both Kaplan and Davies concluded that organized neighborhood opposition groups were most likely to form when the population affected by a proposed project had been relatively stable.[16] However, even the organized site residents will vary considerably in the political resources at their disposal. Leadership is a resource which is crucial if a group is to engage in effective coordinated action. Some groups have natural leaders such as Jane Jacobs who led in the successful battle of a group of Greenwich Village residents against renewal.[17] In the West End area of Boston, however, the residents could not find a leader to mold an effective organization.[18] A good group leader should be well versed in the nature of politics and know how to form crucial coalitions. He should also have access to the news media, and understand where to find the potential resources for the cause. In short, the neighborhood group rarely has a set of ready-made political resources. They must first have a leader who will know where and how to get them. In addition, the neighborhood group must find allies to be influential. In large cities the number of people involved in a clearance project is usually not sufficient to have their vote become a

---

[16]Davies, *op. cit.*, pp. 153, 209; Kaplan, *op. cit.*, p. 136.
[17]Davies, *op. cit.*, pp. 72-109.
[18]Herbert J. Gans, *The Urban Villagers, op. cit.*

particularly important resource. In Newark the opposition of the neighborhood groups to urban renewal was virtually ignored by the city administration.[19]

The Actors and Their Strategies

The distribution of political resources among the actors in the process of slum clearance and redevelopment does not by itself determine how particular actors will fare. Sometimes neighborhood groups are able to block or substantially alter a project proposed by a planner or mayor, while in other instances the planner gets his way. The use of political resources both in the sense of intensity and strategy is very important in determining the outcome of a public policy issue. There are no known patterns in the intensity with which the actors use their resources. Sometimes urban redevelopment has proceeded with virtually no controversy and little political resources expended while other projects have involved major conflict. On the basis of his analysis of renewal in New York, Davies observed that the reaction of citizen groups to a proposed project will be determined by the general reputation of urban renewal, the past experience groups have had with renewal projects, and other issues which affect the neighborhood. If urban renewal projects are reputed to be harmful to site residents and if the residents of the proposed project have been adversely affected by renewal in the past, they are more likely to expend resources to oppose the project. If there are no other issues for which political resources are needed, the citizens will also be more willing to go after the renewal project. Conflict among other actors in the clearance project is more apt to be over details of the proposal rather than over whether or not there should be a project. The intensity with which they use their political resources will be largely determined by the importance which individual actors attach to their stakes in a particular redevelopment project.

The strategies employed by groups and individuals is another important aspect of the use of resources. One strategy common to all actors in an issue over slum clearance and redevelopment is to seek alliances with individuals and groups with common interests in the outcome of that issue. There are certain major areas of agreement among various actors in such an issue. City officials want a project that will bring increased taxes and economic prosperity to the city, while big business wants more profits. Thus they will often agree on a project which will remove slums and replace them with either office

---

[19] Kaplan, *op. cit.*

buildings or middle to upper income housing. The site residents, on the other hand, will want either better housing or the right to stay in their present homes. At times, there will be disagreements within the business community due to the fact that a project will benefit one part of the business district more than others.

Given these broad areas of agreement and disagreement the planners and city officials propose a project which they feel will best suit their objectives as well as those of the most influential elements in the city. There are two kinds of strategies which are generally used in initiating the project. One strategy is to keep the nature of the project a secret until a solid front of agreement from key actors in the project is secured. This was the strategy of the planner in Newark. Before residents of the proposed site area were told that a project was being contemplated, all planning details were worked out and agreed upon by all of the actors with "institutional stakes" in the project. By the time the general public was informed of the plans, formidable support for the project had already been secured.[20] An alternative strategy used by the initiators of redevelopment projects is to keep the general public advised of the city's plans at each step in the planning process. The idea is to meet opposition arguments as the plan is developed and avoid a major battle at a later stage. Kaplan points out that the success of the first kind of strategy depends on a situation where the stakes in renewal are structured sufficiently so that the planners and politicians can foresee opposition and figure out a necessary accommodation. In a less structured situation the second kind of strategy might be more successful.

Those who wish to oppose a redevelopment project also have two major kinds of strategies which they can pursue. One is to obtain access to the political decision-makers and use the political resources at their disposal to pressure them. The other strategy is to use the courts. The taxpayer suit is a fairly common example of the second type of strategy. At the very least it will succeed in stalling the project. If the stall occurs at a crucial time (such as when the developer is about to sign a lease with a big tenant of a proposed development) it can kill the whole project. Not all actors in a slum clearance issue have the money or knowledge to use the courts. They must, therefore, gain access to the decision-makers.

Davies has analyzed how private groups and individuals have attempted to influence governmental officials involved with redevelopment in New York City.[21] He suggests there are two accesses to city

[20]Kaplan, *op. cit.*
[21]Davies, *op. cit.*, pp. 191-204.

officials. The first is to the elected official who is able to communicate the views of his constituents to the appointed members of the bureaucracy and influence what the bureaucrats do. The other is directly to the bureaucrat or technician. In either case, the private group or individual, in order to have good access, must represent an important element in the official's political base. If the planner feels he needs support from the civic boosters club, for example, he will tend to listen more carefully to their opinions. The mayor will listen to those who are regular contributors to his campaign as well as to those who control many votes. Davies points out that city-wide organizations (the chamber of commerce, the news media, civil rights groups, church groups, and business associations) are apt to have greater access than an individual neighborhood association because they represent city-wide interests important to political officials and to the planners. Thus neighborhood organizations often attempt to form alliances with the city-wide organizations. The neighborhood groups will also use their own elected representatives as a means of access to city hall. If these groups are cohesive and represent an important percentage of a constituency, they will be listened to by their elected representatives.

Private organizations employ a number of devices in order to persuade decision-makers that their views are important. Generally they try to attract public attention and sympathy to their cause in order to gain favorable public opinion. This is accomplished through statements to the mass media, letter writing campaigns, appearances and speeches at public meetings. If all else fails, civil disobedience—sit-ins, or refusal to leave homes slated for demolition—will attract considerable attention and will sometimes force city officials to negotiate.

Thus large numbers of groups and individuals with varying stakes in slum clearance and redevelopment use their resources to attempt to influence the plan and its implementation. A variety of strategies can be used by different actors to try to bring about a decision that will benefit them. When resources are being used for different objectives, a state of conflict exists. The effect of a decision which implements a redevelopment project is to resolve or manage the state of conflict in one way or another. The strategy of keeping plans for redevelopment secret until the last minute is one mechanism which many officials use to manage conflict. Another mechanism is compromise. Boundaries of a redevelopment project can be altered or the project may be given a higher or lower priority. The politician may also offer rewards in return for cooperation. For example: a promise of another redevelopment project to constituents who feel that the proposed project will not benefit them; alternatively those forced from their homes might be promised better housing; or constituents with an interest in another issue unrelated to redevelopment might be promised support on that issue from the mayor in return for their support on the redevelopment issue. The politician could also threaten his opposition by promising to withdraw his support for some measure which is of vital importance to his opponents. One final mechanism of conflict management is simply giving in to the demands of a powerful opposition. Plans for an urban redevelopment project might be completely abandoned if the opposition is strong enough. The choice of a conflict management mechanism will depend largely on the politician's assessment of the power of the opposing factions. Most political decision-makers will attempt to develop a redevelopment policy which will generate the greatest benefits for the most powerful interests, while minimizing the disadvantages of redevelopment. The planner, by his own resources, is in a good position to shape the policy which emerges from the conflict. Whatever mechanism of conflict management is used, it is clear that politics is a crucial part of the formulation of planning policy. Professional standards for projects cannot be neutral to all of the interests at stake in the city. Consequently, when conflict arises it must be managed through the political process.

Suburban Planning: Changing the Zoning Ordinance

It was noted that municipalities which are the most "suburban" in character are primarily interested in a planning policy which stresses preservation. At times, however, they find this value challenged by the need for land uses which will help ease their fiscal problems. In fact, the attempt to pursue the preservation objective while satisfying the need for fiscally productive land uses generates an issue which frequently confronts the suburban planner. This involves a different type of politics from that found in the central city. In the case of the city, the most conflict laden planning issues arise when the objectives of the city dwellers clash with the forces wishing to save the downtown economically. In the case of the suburbs, the confrontation over planning is generally between the groups wishing to preserve the status quo and those looking for a larger tax base or some form of economic gain. This confrontation generates a different assortment of actors, stakes and strategies than those found in the slum clearance issue.

The preservation vs. fiscal productivity issue is usually touched off by a proposal to change the zoning ordinance. Such proposals are often made in order to allow the community to accommodate land uses which will yield more taxes than the established single-family homes on large lots. This type of change in the zoning ordinance can be politically explosive.

The planner is a reluctant key figure in the changing of the zoning ordinance. Most planning students are taught that zoning is simply one of the tools available for implementing a plan. The administration of the zoning ordinance is supposed to be a very small part of his work. In reality, the suburban planner spends the major part of his time considering proposed changes in the zoning ordinance. There are two ways that non-governmental actors can try to change the zoning ordinance; one is administrative and the other legislative. Administrative changes in the zoning ordinance are generally made by seeking a variance which would apply to a specific piece of property. To obtain a variance the property owner should be able to satisfy the administrators that the ordinance imposes some unnecessary hardships or practical difficulty in using his property. Generally, requests for a variance are presented to a board of zoning appeals and the planner is called upon to make his recommendation on the request. If the petitioner is not satisfied by the action of the board, he may take his case to the courts.

Legislative changes in the zoning ordinance involve amending the ordinance. Under this procedure a citizen may petition the municipal legislative body to consider his amendment. Again, the planner is called upon to make his recommendation to the council. The amendment can be contested in the courts but it must be demonstrated that the proposed change benefits either the entire municipality or the neighborhood in which the property is located. Otherwise the amendment can be judged an instance of illegal "spot zoning."

It is beyong the scope of the present discussion to get into a legal analysis of zoning. Our concern is with the emergence and resolution of conflict that often accompany a petition for a change in the zoning ordinance. Thus the focus of this discussion will be on the events occurring when an application is made for an amendment to the existing zoning ordinance. The kinds of proposed changes which generally provoke the greatest conflict are those which propose that a single-family residential zone be altered for other uses.

Actors and Their Stakes

As in the case of slum clearance, a change in the zoning ordinance automatically involves a number of actors who have institutional stakes in the proceedings. Zoning changes will almost always begin with a petitioner or group of petitioners, generally property owners, who are requesting the change in order to develop land in a manner that is not allowed by the existing zoning ordinance. Depending on whether the change sought is an amendment or a variance, a number of municipal officials will be involved. In the case of an amendment, the city council and the mayor or manager are automatically actors. When a variance is sought, the zoning enforcement officer (either the planner or the building inspector) and members of the board of zoning appeals are included in the proceedings. In either kind of zoning change the planner is usually called upon to evaluate the proposed change and to then make a recommendation to the council or board. It is then the usual practice to hold a public hearing on the matter, allowing all interested parties to speak. Council or the board then makes the decision.

The planner has the major professional stakes in proceedings to change the zoning ordinance. He is constantly subjected to the professional view that zoning is a tool for implementing plans and nothing more. For this reason the professional stake in a proposed change in the ordinance is to ascertain that the change will not violate the spirit of the plan and will be in the best interests of the entire community. These professional principles are very difficult to apply to a specific proposed change in the zoning ordinance. As Babcock points out, the planner's professional position in zoning issues is quite ambiguous.[22] When a commercial or industrial use is involved, the planner's decision alters the pattern of competition in the areas i.e. some parties will benefit and others will lose out. The precise benefit-cost impact of a specific change in the zoning ordinance is extremely difficult to determine. If the proposed change involves housing, the planner is faced with a social question. The municipality may wish to exclude Negroes. In this case the planner must ask himself what community his plans are supposed to benefit; should he consider the municipality or the entire metropolis? Thus the planner, while having professional stakes in the outcome of zoning proceedings, is sometimes at a loss to determine how the outcome will affect his interests.

The mayor or manager and councilmen have considerable political stakes in many proposals to change the zoning ordinance. The elected governmental officials in a suburban municipality are expected to help preserve the suburban character of the community. At the same time they must provide the level of public services which the citizens

---

[22]Richard F. Babcock, *The Zoning Game: Municipal Practices and Policies* (Madison: University of Wisconsin Press, 1966), pp. 62-86.

demand. Given these diverse voter expectations, a change in the zoning ordinance can be very tricky politically. In one suburb of Detroit, some city officials decided that the zoning ordinance should permit industry in the community for tax reasons. A number of residents who lived near the proposed industrial site began proceedings to have the officials recalled partly because they felt the industry would attract Negroes. Other citizens who were concerned about their taxes, however, supported the officials.[23] In a community where the local legislators are elected by wards, the councilman will take a very close look at the political ramifications of a proposed change in the zoning in his ward.

Power and prestige is often at stake in zoning issues. Elected officials, while desiring to return to office, also wish to show their constituents that they can take a position and make it stick. The planner too, puts his personal prestige and that of his office on the line when he makes his recommendation to the council. Often the citizen proposing the change or opposing it finds his prestige in the community is at stake as soon as he makes his request to council.

Economic stakes are very important in zoning issues. The developer or private individual who wants the zoning ordinance changed, usually makes his request for economic reasons. In some cases he wishes to alter his house so that he can run a business of some kind. Alternatively he may wish to build a large commercial center or apartment complex which will bring him economic gain. The development of a new commercial establishment will alter the pattern of competition in the area. Thus other businessmen will have economic stakes in the zoning change. Similarly if an apartment complex is envisioned, the real estate market conditions will be altered, involving the economic interests of residential property owners. The city administration has definite economic interests in zoning. The proposed use of the property to be rezoned will impose certain costs on the city. A big apartment complex, for example, may place a greater load on the local schools. A commercial center or an industrial development will require an increase in expenditures for such services as police and fire protection, garbage and refuse disposal, water supply, etc. Thus both the city administration and taxpayers whose taxes may be affected, will have economic stakes in the proposed development. At the same time, the proposal may also generate additional revenues for the city. For this reason it becomes necessary to look at both the cost and the revenue implications of the proposal in order to determine how the community

---

[23]Deil Wright, "Livonia Adopts a Zoning Ordinance." Unpublished case study.

will be affected fiscally. It is possible that while a development may favorably affect the city's finances, it will hurt the property values of the land around it. Thus the owners of the affected property will have an economic stake in the zoning proposal. The same is true if the property values are favorably affected. For all of these reasons the economic stakes in a proposed change in the zoning ordinance may be considerable.

Babcock has suggested that in suburbia the social stakes in the zoning ordinance are usually the most important of all.[24] He has observed that suburban communities are extremely reluctant to accept housing developments which contain anything more than the free-standing single-family homes. Apartments, townhouses or cluster developments are often rejected because of the fear that such developments will allow city dwellers to live in their community or that they will create an unfavorable image.[25] Commercial centers and "clean" industries, on the other hand are often accepted for their presumed economic benefit. Certain kinds of non-residential establishments, however, will be opposed if they are considered a source of employment for low-income people or if they are apt to tarnish the social image of the community. In one community the residents were opposed to the development of a motel near the local school because the residents felt that motels catered to immoral behavior which would corrupt their children on their way to and from school![26] Likewise, an industrial establishment which employs blue collar workers may be unacceptable in spite of any economic benefits it would bring. These social stakes in the zoning ordinance are apt to generate an intense reaction to certain proposed zoning changes.

The ideological stakes in zoning questions are probably less prevalent than those associated with slum clearance and redevelopment. Most suburbanites now support zoning in principal. In a sense, social attitudes concerning the desirability of maintaining a particular social mixture in the community as well as a "suburban image" is an ideological and a social stake in zoning.

The stakes in changing suburban zoning ordinances are the same as those in central city slum clearance projects, but the context of these stakes is quite different. Slightly fewer actors are involved in zoning since the communities are smaller and the formal decision-making process less complex. Planners, elected municipal officials, real estate

---

[24]Babcock, *op. cit.*, pp. 30-38, 43-61.
[25]This is particularly true when proposed rents are moderate to low.
[26]Wright, *op. cit.*, pp. 33-36.

developers, local businessmen, and a large number of private citizens will none-the-less be involved with zoning questions. The political resources available to each actor are similar to those discussed in connection with slum clearance in the city.

Actors and Their Strategies

The strategies employed by actors involved with an amendment to a zoning ordinance are fairly straight forward. The developer or owner of the property which is being considered for rezoning may use his money and prestige in a variety of ways. He is required to make a formal proposal to council proving that the proposed use of the land in question will benefit either the entire municipality or the neighborhood in which it is located. He may go to the planner before making this proposal and attempt to gain the planner's aid and support. He may also go to certain other influential public officials and key private citizens. In addition he may solicit the support of the suburban press. If, prior to his formal request to the council, the petitioner can gain the support of the planner and other key people, the decision concerning his proposal can be wrapped up before other interested citizens get into the proceedings. If all else fails, the developer can appeal to the courts on the grounds that the zoning ordinance discriminates against him.

The planner may also utilize different strategies. Generally there is a period of time between the developer's initial request for a change in the zoning ordinance and the planner's recommendation on that request. If the planner agrees with the proposal and sees little reason for opposition to it, he will simply make his recommendation to council, either privately or at the public hearing, giving the reasons for his support. If he sees that there will be disagreement over his recommendation, he may try to persuade members of the council and the mayor on an informal basis. His professional skills and training are his major political resources in these cases. He pits these skills against the economic claims of the developer and argues that his position represents the public interest. The planner may actually hold special meetings with interested citizens to explain why he takes the position he does. The planner's professional skills and training, however, are not very effective political resources in this situation. As Babcock points out, many citizens feel that their judgment is as good as the planner's and that no serious repercussions will result if the planner's advice is not followed.[27] At worst, the citizen can always go to live

---

[27]Babcock, *op. cit.*, pp. 64-65.

in another suburb if a failure to follow the planner's advice substantially hurts the municipality. For these reasons, the planner often finds himself either seeking consensus before the battle begins or coming out on the losing side of the argument.

The elected city official will generally follow the sentiments of the majority in a zoning dispute. Where the zoning change involves crucial fiscal questions and is unpopular with the citizens, the politicians will first try to find respected people in the community to speak for the measure at a public hearing. If the hearing indicates strong opposition, a favorite ploy is to refer the matter back to the planner for "further study." Often the planner becomes the goat in an unpopular zoning decision. The politician may take the position that he must rely on his professional staff for technical advice and his planner feels that the zoning ordinance should be changed. In this manner he can soften criticism directed toward him by suggesting that he is simply taking the advice of his planner who evaluates zoning matters from a professional point of view and in the interest of the public as a whole.

Suburban citizens who wish to influence a zoning decision have easier access to the government than do the neighborhood groups in the central city, because of the smaller size of the suburb. Another reason is the "grass roots" democratic ideal that is prevalent in many suburban communities. Suburban people expect easy and direct access to elected officials and they often get it. Thus meetings with the mayor can be set up where citizens can express themselves informally on an important zoning question. The strategy of citizens groups or of individuals seems to be more personal in the suburbs. Petitions are circulated, phone calls to the councilman or mayor are made, local newspaper ads are run. If the papers are not favorable to a group's cause, it is not uncommon for the group to publish a newsletter and distribute it widely in the community. At times these newsletters simply explain a group's position while at other times they try to scare people into coming to the public hearing and speaking up to the councilmen. One newsletter, for example, claimed that a proposed change in the zoning ordinance would bring factories into the nicest residential neighborhoods. The public hearing on the zoning change is the forum where the most vigorous citizen involvement takes place. Citizen groups are often organized so that speeches at the hearing are arranged ahead of time. Hearings sometimes become unruly shouting matches where various parties to the dispute all try to air their views at once. When this occurs, the council will often delay the hearings to another time. Thus groups wishing to stall the question may go to the hearing simply to make noise. The citizen can also go to the courts and protest an amendment on the grounds that it is not in accordance with the local plan and that it will cause him to suffer economic losses.

These same strategies are also used by the actors in a zoning issue when a variance rather than an amendment to the zoning ordinance is sought. In this case the body holding the hearing is the zoning board of appeals rather than the council. The outcome of zoning issues, short of court action, is not necessarily determined by professional planning standards. As noted earlier, application of planning standards to proposals to change the zoning ordinance are difficult at best. Furthermore, other actors who become involved with the zoning issue often pay little attention to the planner if their views differ from his. Zoning ordinances of growing communities are usually riddled with variances and amendments. This is partially a reflection of the fact that the zoning ordinance is a hopelessly static document in a dynamic environment of urban change. In addition, the frequent changes in zoning ordinances are testimony to the fact that individual stakes are involved in any plan that might be made and that some of these stakes are usually at odds with others. Thus, changing the zoning ordinance generates conflict and the need for conflict management.

The mechanisms used by suburban politicians to manage conflict over zoning questions are not too different from those used in central city redevelopment issues. Compromise on a zoning change is difficult because so many zoning questions lack a middle ground. But promises of reward or threats can be made. It is also possible to change other portions of a zoning ordinance in addition to that being requested which may be helpful to some group or another. The most prominant conflict management mechanism has already been mentioned. The blame for any unpopular decision can be shifted to the planner which will mute any resulting hostilities toward the politician.

Conclusion

The generation and management of conflict—either actual or potential—is a key aspect of the formulation of planning policy, involving a transformation of human values into legally binding public policy. Since all groups and individuals in our society do not share common values, planning and politics cannot be separated. The precise manner in which the planner's technical and value judgments are transformed into public policy depends on which actors become involved in the decision-making process, what stakes they have in the outcome of that process, the political resources which they possess and the way in which they use them. The interaction of actors, stakes, resources, and strategies is greatly influenced by metropolitanism. The issues connected with slum clearance and redevelopment are typical of the kinds of human value differences which affect the planning process in the central city prototype. For this reason we used slum clearance as a means of illustrating some of the general concepts which make up the subject matter of the politics of planning. Likewise in the suburban community prototype, a change in the zoning ordinance illustrates the kinds of issues which face the planner. This analysis has not attempted to generalize about the kinds of circumstances which are apt to produce stakes in planning policy. Some hypotheses concerning these circumstances are developed in the following chapter. These hypotheses deal generally with the politics of planning and do not relate directly to our concern with metropolitan areas.

Determinants of Political Involvement in Planning

7

The stakes which groups and individuals have in a planning issue, their political resources and the way in which they use their resources provide a framework for analyzing the scope of political involvement and the conflict which a given planning issue may generate.[1] Another level of analysis is needed, however, to understand why the stakes and resources involved in the planning process vary from issue to issue and from community to community. At this level we need to ask what variables explain variations in the stakes and resources that are affected by planning issues? Five variables (called here the determinants of political involvement in planning) have been chosen for the present discussion. It is believed that they are the most significant variables in terms of their ability to enhance our understanding of the politics of planning. They are: the dimensions of planning policy, local political culture, the role played by the planner, community power structures, and community socio-economic characteristics.

The Dimensions of Planning Policy

Planning differs from other functions of local government in a very significant way. While police, fire and other traditional activities of

[1]It should be noted here that a single planning policy proposal may actually raise a number of separate issues to a variety of different actors.

local government have a clearly defined scope of activity, planning does not. The content of the municipal planner's work varies considerably from agency to agency. Also within many agencies there are numerous things which the planners are doing. In short, planning policy can have many different dimensions. By considering the dimensions of planning policy as a determinant of political involvement in planning, it is suggested that the nature of the planner's work itself is an important aspect of the politics of planning. For this reason the various dimensions of planning policy are described and some hypotheses are presented which are addressed to the following questions. How does the nature of the planning function affect political participation in the formulation of planning policy? How does it affect the likelihood that the planner's recommendations will be acceptable to political decision-makers? There are four dimensions of planning policy that seem relevant to these questions: time, the subject matter of planning, the scope of planning decisions, and the nature of the public commitments which such decisions require.

All planning is concerned with the future. However, some planning policies are directed to events which will occur almost immediately while other policies are concerned with the more distant future. Thus, in terms of time, planning policy can be short or long range. The long-range policy could extend anywhere from a year to a hundred years. The criterion used here for classifying policy as long-range is not the actual time between policy and action but the subjective judgment of the general public and the elected public officials that action resulting from a policy is not imminent. We can call the formulation of long-range planning policy "plan making activity." The short-range classification of planning policy involves decisions based on policies which have already been made and which will lead to concrete and immediate (using the subjective criterion) action. The formulation of policy in this category can be called "implementation activity." Examples of implementation activity would include specific plans for the physical layout of an urban renewal project; the writing and administration of zoning ordinances, subdivision controls and building codes; and the coordination of governmental activity including capital budgeting. The time dimension of planning policy might best be conceived as a continuum rather than as two categories. But politically, planning policy falls into one of the two classifications described above. Implementation activity has very different political implications from plan making activity and the political stakes in the outcome are more readily identified. Potential actors are most apt to become involved when the resolution of an issue will result in immediate action. Thus as the potential actors become active over an issue, the political stakes in that issue become clear. In addition, political decision-makers have some knowledge of the existing distribution of political stakes and resources. With this knowledge they can assess the consequences of policies which will result in immediate action. But plan making activity requires the formulation of policies which do not require action until some time in the future. This creates some problems for the decision-maker. First, it becomes more difficult to determine what the immediate political consequences of his decisions will be. Many of the potential actors will not become involved until that time when the policy is to be put into effect. Second, it is hard for the politician to know what the future political implications of his decision will be, since the whole structure of actors, stakes and resources will change. Thus the time dimension has a considerable affect on the degree of political uncertainty connected with planning. Uncertainty is greatest for the plan making activity. For this reason the political acceptability of the long range planning policy will depend largely on the other three dimensions of planning.

The subject matter of plans is one of these dimensions and varies considerably. In Chapter 1 we suggested that most plans made by local planning agencies focus on physical development. However, even these plans vary in the extent to which they consider social and economic development as a by-product. In addition, the physical plans also differ in the extent to which they involve activities of other departments and agencies of the government. A plan for streets and highways, for example, would involve the street and highway department of a municipality. Furthermore, the subject matter of the plan can go beyond physical development and cover practically everything the government is doing. Such a plan would be what Fagin and others have called the "policies plan."[2] It would consider the quality of education, the nature of social welfare services, etc. Conceptually, we can classify plans along a continuum with plans which consider only physical development at one end and the policies plan the other end. As plans deal with broader subject matter they will be classified closer to the policies plan end of the continuum.

Another dimension of planning is the scope of the decisions that are required by the plan. This dimension can also be described in terms of a continuum. At one end of this continuum is the plan that calls only for very marginal changes in existing policies or incremen-

[2]Henry Fagin, "Organizing and Carrying Out Planning Activities Within Urban Government," *Journal of the American Institute of Planners* (August, 1957), pp. 109-114.

tal decisions. To illustrate: suppose that we are looking at that part of the plan which deals with traffic. An incremental decision concerning traffic would be directed toward one or more specific traffic problems such as the daily traffic jam during rush hours at a particular intersection of streets. The solution might be to make some streets one way or to synchronize traffic signals. At the other end of the continuum would be the very broad sweeping decisions. Using the traffic situation as an example, a broad sweeping decision might require that the entire metropolitan area transportation system be changed by building new highways and mass transit facilities. Thus an incremental decision calls for only marginal changes in the status quo while the broad sweeping decision calls for extensive changes.

A final dimension of planning involves the nature of the commitments which the plan requires the elected officials to make. This dimension adds another continuum to our model. At one end is the very vague or general commitment i.e. "The city will take measures to solve the traffic problem." At the other end of the continuum are very specific commitments such as "The city will solve the traffic problem by building a major mass transit system with stations at the following locations . . . and whose tracks will run along the following route. . . ."

These three dimensions–subject matter, scope of decision, and nature of commitment–can be combined into a single three dimension model. In Figure 2 the three continua have been drawn with each bisecting one another at right angles. The combined model has then been enclosed in a cube. Any plan can be represented as a point falling within the cube. Each of the heavy lines within the cube represent one of the continua discussed above. Line *ab* represents the subject matter of planning with point *a* being the completely physical plan and point *b* representing the policies plan. Line *cd* is the continuum indicating the scope of decisions with point *c* as the incremental decision; point *d* the broad, sweeping decision. Line *ef* is the continuum which illustrates the specificity of commitment which will be required of political decision-makers if they adopt the plan. Point *e* requires only very general commitments while point *f* involves the very specific.

This diagram illustrates the range of different plans that could be developed. There are an almost infinite number of combined positions along the three continua in which a plan may fall. Point Z is the meeting place of points *b*, *d*, and *f*. A plan classified as Z would be one dealing with all public policies, calling for very extensive changes and requiring very specific commitments. A plan classified as X (the meeting place of points *a*, *c*, and *e*) is at the other extreme. This plan deals only with the physical environment, involves only incremental decisions and very vague and general commitments. A few other combinations are also illustrated on the diagram. Point Y, where a_1, c_1, and e_1 meet, is a plan that strongly emphasizes the physical

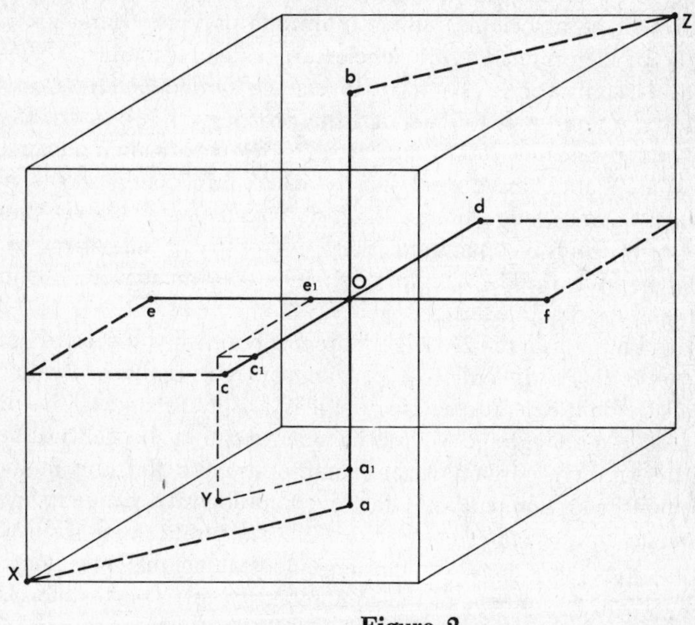

Figure 2

A Model of the Dimensions of Planning Policy

environment, involves decisions that tend to be incremental and requires a moderate degree of specific commitments. Point O would characterize plans which fall at the midpoint of each continuum.

This model is a convenient way to illustrate how the type of planning which the local planning agency is doing influences the politics of planning. Plan Z is the extreme example of comprehensive planning. It also has the least likelihood of being adopted or implemented intact. In the first place, plan Z has the greatest potential for extensive conflict (extensive is used here in a quantitative sense.) As the plan becomes more comprehensive and specific, the number of people and stakes affected by the plan increases. Because of the negative bias in planning, greater political participation in the planning process is apt to mean a less cheerful prospect for the plan itself remaining intact. It is true that a very narrowly conceived plan can generate intensive conflict. But that conflict will tend to center around a specific issue, while the broader plan will generate conflict over a number of issues.

A second reason the probability for the political survival of plan Z is low, is that it raises many political questions that cannot be easily answered by either the planner or the politician. Any existing public policy will be associated with a multitude of vested interests which cannot be determined until policies are actually changed. Thus the political ramifications of a plan to change public policy is often an unknown quantity. It follows that the broader the scope of the plan, the greater the uncertainties relative to the political implications of that plan. Politicians do not like to make firm commitments in the absence of knowledge of the interests which are at stake. Thus the most comprehensive plans will tend to receive a lukewarm to cold reception from the decision-makers, since they must bear the burden of any adverse political consequences.

Plans falling into the Z category are not politically attractive because they tend to be difficult to reconcile with the realities of our local pluralistic political system. This point is closely related to the discussion above. Banfield and Wilson have argued that the political system operates through bargaining and compromise and that this method of operation is not compatible with the comprehensive planners' ideal of implementing sweeping conceptions of "the public interest."[3] Altshuler makes a much more detailed argument along the same lines.[4] He suggests that acceptance of the comprehensive plan makes the planner an arbitrator among all the conflicting interests that are touched by the plan's content. The plan itself is, by definition, based on either conscious or unconscious goals. The comprehensive plan presents the planner-arbitrator with two difficulties. First, he must develop criteria that can be a basis for policies that will meet the goals. But at the present time, the planners' knowledge of the interrelationships among policy areas is not really sufficient to develop criteria for policies that are very broad. Secondly, Altshuler argues that the justification for having the planner in the role of arbitrator is contingent on the existence of a community-wide consensus (on some goals). Conflict must thus be considered as minor disagreement over the means to commonly held ends. In Minneapolis and St. Paul, however, Altshuler found that the planners were not even able to have a sustained discussion of goals. Furthermore, in a pluralistic political system the

---

[3]Edward Banfield and James Q. Wilson, *City Politics* (Cambridge, Mass.: M.I.T. Press and Harvard University Press, 1963), pp. 202-203.

[4]Alan Altshuler, *The City Planning Process* (Ithaca: Cornell University Press, 1966), pp. 299-332.

planner is not likely to find agreement even if a public discussion of goals could be set up. Thus the planner cannot, according to Altshuler, justify an arbitrator's role for himself. If commonly held ends cannot be found, the political decision-maker who can bargain and compromise must be the arbitrator.

The Altshuler argument is a convincing one. It applies mainly to plans which are classified in our model as Z or those quite close to Z. Plans of the X variety do not generate as much of a political problem because they can be based on a very limited set of objectives which can more easily be determined. Thus agreement or consensus is more likely. Generally speaking, therefore, planning activity which does not involve immediate action, which involves a broad range of subject matter, which requires broad sweeping changes and which also requires specific policy commitments from politicians is the least likely to survive. Such plans have the greatest potential for conflict in a quantitative sense. They are full of uncertainties concerning their political ramifications and are the most difficult to reconcile with the character of our local political system. Thus the dimensions of planning policy are important determinants of political involvement in planning.

Political Culture

Another factor which can affect the politics of planning is the political culture of a community. Generally, the term political culture refers to the predominant expectations which the people in a community have relative to the things government ought to be doing.[5] Applied to planning, political culture affects how the residents of a community feel about planning as a function of government. In many instances the political culture may effectively limit what the planner can do.

In the United States as a whole, planning is generally accepted as a proper function of local government. This has not always been the case. Planning in earlier times was rejected as being inconsistent with the predominant liberal interpretation of freedom and democracy. Under this interpretation, freedom meant a minimum of public interference with private activities and institutions. Planning at the national level still is stigmatized by being associated with socialism or even communism. Thus planning at the national level is not called plan-

[5]Banfield and Wilson, *op. cit.*, pp. 58-60.

ning. At the local level, however, most people today do not feel that planning is inconsistent with democracy. This attitude is probably due to the fact that local planning in its earliest stages was advocated by highly reputable people in local communities and was associated with political reform.[6] In short, planning at the local level was presented to the American people as a possible solution to the very visible and serious problems of cities which the private market had not been able to control.

While the political culture of the United States as a whole generally supports planning as a function of local government, the degree of acceptance will vary from community to community. Altshuler, for example, found political culture differences between Minneapolis and St. Paul which seemed to affect the planning function.[7] Minneapolis appeared to have a less favorable climate for planning than St. Paul as a result of early experiences with a planning director. Many Minneapolis people also tended to associate planning with Federal urban redevelopment and socialism. Alternatively in Berkeley, California, planning seems to enjoy very favorable acceptance.[8] One further example of differences in political culture is provided by Oliver Williams who developed a typology of middle-sized cities according to the residents' expectations about the appropriate role of local government.[9] The cities examined by Williams viewed government in a number of ways: as an instrument of community growth, as a provider of amenities, as a caretaker, and as an arbiter of conflicting interests.

It is difficult to pin down the reasons for differences in political culture. Attitudes toward the planning function may be shaped by such variables as the length of time the planning function has been established in a community, the experience the community residents have had with planning and planners in the past, and the strength of laissez-faire sentiment in the community. One hypothesis about local political behavior which could serve as a partial explanation for differences in political culture links socio-economic characteristics of the

---

[6]Alan K. Campbell, "A Political Science Approach to Planning Change," *Planning Socio-Economic Change* (Raleigh, North Carolina: Agricultural Policy Institute, October, 1964), pp. 57-69.

[7]Altshuler, *op. cit.*, Chapters II and IV.

[8]On the basis of reading the Altshuler case studies and other case studies of planning in Berkeley by Warren Campbell, this writer concluded that political culture in Berkeley is more favorable to planning than is the case in either Minneapolis or St. Paul.

[9]Oliver Williams, "A Typology for Comparative Local Government," *Midwest Journal of Political Science* (May, 1961), pp. 150-164.

population to attitudes about the role of government.[10] Banfield and Wilson argue that there are two kinds of discernable political ethos. One is derived primarily from Anglo-Saxon Protestant values which Banfield and Wilson have termed a "public regarding" view of government. This public regarding ethos suggests that government should do those things which will benefit the community "as a whole." According to Banfield and Wilson, middle and upper-class people tend to have such an outlook. The other ethos have been termed "private regarding." It grew out of European political experience which did not include a tradition of independent political action. Immigrants from the Western European countries have viewed the role of government in very personal terms. They have placed a higher value on personal gain from the system than on any conception of a public interest. Thus, those subscribing to the private regarding ethos tend to look to government as a source of personal benefit. Banfield and Wilson hypothesize that in the United States the very wealthy aristocracy and the low-income groups generally subscribe to the private regarding ethos.

The public and private regarding hypothesis has interesting implications for the politics of planning. Planning is clearly based on a public regarding view of government. The plan is supposed to be a future conception of the public interest. Planning theory frowns on any planning policy which is contaminated by influence from special groups. Thus if a community is largely made up of groups which subscribe to a public regarding ethos, the planning activities will generally have a better chance of achieving their aims than in communities where private regarding views are predominant.

The Role of the Planner

The role which the planner chooses to play in the politics of planning can influence both the extent to which planning issues will generate conflict and the way in which conflicts are resolved. The planner has several alternative roles which he can play. He can be a political agnostic who makes his recommendations strictly on a "profes-

---

[10]Banfield and Wilson, *City Politics, op. cit.* For a critique of the Banfield-Wilson hypothesis see Raymond E. Wolfinger and John Osgood Field, "Political Ethos and the Structure of City Government," *American Political Science Review* (June, 1966). A further exchange between Banfield-Wilson and Wolfinger-Field is found in the "Communications" of *American Political Science Review* (December, 1966), pp. 998-1000.

sional" basis without any thought about the political acceptability of his proposals. Alternatively, he can assume the role of confidential advisor to the political decision-maker by shaping planning recommendations so they are in accord with the politician's desire to be re-elected. Finally, the planner can be a political activist, making decisions based on "professional" criteria and then taking to the stump to drum up political support from the community-at-large. By playing this role the planner is always trying to sell his proposals to the politician. While some planners may play one of these roles to the exclusion of the others, most planners play all of these roles at one time or another.

There is no consistent normative theory of planning which could serve as a guide to professional planners in choosing one of the alternatives. As we have noted, early planners thought planning should be kept out of politics. There is some very limited evidence that this belief still persists and that the political agnostic role still finds a number of adherents. A survey of planning students at the Massachusetts Institute of Technology, for example, indicated that 61 per cent of those interviewed thought that politicians were "unprofessional."[11] The survey also indicated that the planning students thought the objectives of the planner and the politician were far apart. The students felt that planners were engaged in rational decision-making to serve society's interest, while the politicians were engaged in "irrational" decision-making to serve selfish interests.

Other surveys cited by Rabinovitz provide some notions about the role played by practicing planners.[12] When asked why they had entered the planning field the planners' answers suggest that the desire to be a "professional" and job security were foremost in their minds. Such motivations would not necessarily produce political agnostics. However, the desire for job security and the ideology of "professionalism" may cause planners to alter their activities and ideas in order to avoid conflict. Altshuler found that planners in Minneapolis and St. Paul tried to avoid conflict by avoiding controversial issues.[13] He concluded that planners are caught in a dilemma because of an inherent conflict between their attitudes and their tendency to

---

[11]Francine F. Rabinovitz, "Politics, Personality and Planning," *Public Administration Review* (March, 1967), pp. 18-24.

[12]The surveys cited were originally presented by Robert Daland and John Parker, "Roles of the Planner in Urban Development," in F. S. Chapin and S. Weiss, *Urban Growth Dynamics* (New York: John Wiley & Sons, 1962); also John Dyckman, "What Makes Planners Plan," *Journal of the American Institute of Planners* (May, 1961), pp. 164-167.

[13]Altshuler, *op. cit.*, Chapters VII and VIII.

equate successful planning with plan implementation. Their professional attitudes require that they should present the public with crucial alternatives, but they are afraid to risk political defeat by letting the public and the politicians know that there are any technical uncertainties in the subject matter of their plans. Secondly, the planner is committed to a comprehensive plan which recognizes complex interrelationships among the consequences of planning policy. The Minneapolis and St. Paul planners felt that their proposals would not be politically attractive under these circumstances because potential controversy would be heightened.[14]

Planners and students of planning who have written about the role of the planner have not come to any clear and consistent conclusions. While traditional planning ideology supports the political agnostic view, more recent literature has suggested that the planner ought to be recommending courses of action which are acceptable both to planning practice and to the politicians' political careers. Walker was an early advocate of this course of action.[15] And more recently Charles Ascher has strongly suggested such a role for the planner.[16] Nash and Shurtleff have argued that if there are strong points of disagreement between the planner and the political decision-makers it is up to the planner to resign.[17] With the possible exception of the Nash-Shurtleff article, there are no guidelines which indicate what the planner should do when he disagrees with the politicians. As Altshuler suggests, the planning profession has no normative theory to use as a guide in this difficulty.

Because there is no normative theory planners assume varying roles. While there is no data that indicates which of the three roles—agnostic, confidant, or activist—is played most often, casual observation would suggest that all three have been played at one time or another by different professional planners. The effect of playing one role or the other on the politics of planning is not well established but some reasonable hypotheses can be presented. The political agnostic will generally have the least success in having his proposals implemented. He will tend not only to ignore the needs of the politicians but will often be hostile to these needs. Under these cirum-

---

[14]*Ibid.*, p. 392.

[15]Robert A. Walker, *op. cit.*

[16]Charles S. Ascher, "City Planning Administration—and Politics," *Land Economics* (1954), pp. 320-328.

[17]Peter H. Nash and James F. Shurtleff, "Planning As a Staff Function in Urban Management," *Journal of the American Institute of Planners* (Summer, 1954), pp. 136-147.

stances plans will be apt to reflect the planner's individual concept of the public interest. If his schemes call for broad sweeping changes and specific commitments from the politician without being sensitive to that politician's needs, the planner will generally be ignored. Obviously the planner who plays the role of political confidant will have a far greater chance of seeing his proposals implemented. This success may be due to the fact that the planning proposals will be altered to such an extent that they will cause no ripples in the political waters. However, such success may also reflect the ability of the planner to come up with and sell realistic yet meaningful proposals. The political activist's chances of success could go either way. By assuming the activist role, he places his job in jeopardy. In addition, the risks of alienating the political decision-makers in the process of playing the game of winning support for his program are great. On the other hand, many planners do possess important political resources such as information about the community and an ability to get Federal grants. These resources can make him very influential. However, because of the risks and a lack of knowledge of how to use these resources, few planners are playing the activist role.

Community Power Structures

The distribution of power among various segments of the community can have a decisive influence on the outcome of planning issues and may determine which issues will be publicly aired. The possession of political resources is a key element in measuring the influence of an individual or group over public policy. In spite of the fact that elected governmental officials have considerable formal powers which are important political resources, a large number of studies have been made which stress the influence of non-governmental people and groups through informal means. Some of these studies of "community power structures" have underplayed the role of the formal government to such an extent that they have given the impression that all decisions are actually made "behind the scenes" by a small elite group of people.

This description of local political behavior gained widespread attention through Floyd Hunter's study of Atlanta.[18] He found there were a relatively small number (40) of community influentials who essentially used the government as a legitimate bureaucracy to carry out

---

[18]Floyd Hunter, *Community Power Structure* (Chapel Hill: University of North Carolina Press, 1953).

the decisions they had made. His finding became representative of a certain school of thought which holds that power structures are "monolithic." That is, small influential groups make policy on all important issues faced by local government. The findings of a study by Robert Dahl are much different from Hunter's and represent an alternative theory of the nature of community power.[19] This theory holds that power is "polylithic." The proponents of the polylithic theory contend that different groups are involved in different policy issues depending upon the nature of those issues. According to this theory, there is no *single* elite group that formulates all public policy but rather, a variety of private citizens and groups are influential in community decision-making. In the present section we shall explore the relevance of the diverse findings of these and other studies of community power to the politics of planning. Three questions are important to this discussion: Is there *a* structure of power in local communities? What is the relationship between the political power wielded by nongovernmental actors and the power of the governmental actors? How might the structure of power in a community influence the formulation of planning policy?

The two opposing views of community power—monolithic versus polylithic—have sometimes been stated as either/or propositions. Proponents of the two theoretical positions have argued bluntly that they were right and that their critics were wrong. The differences in the findings of various power structure studies have often been explained away by criticism of the methods which the various researchers used.[20] Hunter, for example, has been roundly criticized for the method he used. Having compiled a list of leaders in various aspects of community life, Hunter asked a panel of "long-time, well-informed residents" to narrow down his list by telling who the community's most important people were. He compiled a list of 40 people who, for the most part, were employed in the fields of banking, commerce, and law. The main criticism of Hunter's method has been that he found what he was looking for because of the way he phrased his questions. If you ask people who the "biggest man in town" is, they will generally think of somebody. Further, it is argued that what Hunter found was a list of people with a reputation for being powerful and that

---

[19]Robert A. Dahl, *Who Governs?: Democracy and Power in an American City* (New Haven: Yale University Press, 1961).

[20]For a critical analysis of a variety of power structure studies see Nelson Polsby, *Community Power and Political Theory* (New Haven: Yale University Press, 1963). A good annoted bibliography of the power structure literature between 1950 and 1962 may be found in Charles Press, *Main Street Politics: Policy Making at the Local Level* (East Lansing, Michigan: Institute for Community Development, Michigan State University, 1962).

there is very little evidence presented that these people actually had used this power. Dahl's study of New Haven has also been criticized for the methods used although the criticism has been less than that directed at Hunter. Dahl picked specific issues which he felt had been important in New Haven and then determined who had been the most influential in deciding the outcome of these issues. He found that different sets of people were involved in the issues studied. The major criticism of Dahl's analysis is that he may have prejudiced his findings with the issues he chose to examine. A study of Syracuse by Linton Freeman and others tried to escape this criticism by establishing criteria for selecting decisions that would be representative of important community issues.[21] Altogether 39 different decisions were selected and used to find leadership patterns within the community. Freeman's findings were similar to Dahl's.

Aside from charges of inadequate research methods, differences in the findings of studies of local decision-making have also been attributed to the distinct possibility that there are a variety of power structures in the United States. Some students of local politics have asserted that we ought to attempt to isolate the reasons for the differences which have been discovered. The level of economic development, the heterogeneity of the population, community size, historical factors, and the strength of political parties are among the variables that have been mentioned as possible reasons why power structures might vary. Most studies, with a few exceptions, have concentrated on a single community creating a lack of comparative data on which to base a strong theory of community power.[22]

There are a few generalizations which may be deduced from the findings of the various power structure studies. One such generalization is that only a very small percentage of the population participates in the formulation of public policy of any sort. This has held true even in those communities that have described the power structure as polylithic. In Dahl's study, the total number of influentials in all of the issues he chose were less than one per cent of the populace. Freeman found less than three-tenths of one per cent involved in the 39 issues

---

[21]Linton Freeman, Warner Bloomberg, *et al., Local Community Leadership* (Syracuse: University College, 1960). Also a follow-up to the 1960 study was completed. Linton Freeman, Warner Bloomberg, *et al., Metropolitan Decision Making* (Syracuse: University College, 1962). Bloomberg is presently completing a study of community decision making in the Milwaukee area which will be published soon.

[22]A notable exception is Robert E. Agger, Daniel Goldrich, and Bert E. Swanson, *The Rulers and the Ruled* (New York: John Wiley & Sons, 1964). In this study four communities are compared.

he looked at. The fact that so few people participate in local public policy formulation has led some observers to wonder whether the old monolithic-polylithic argument has much meaning. A second generalization (which is a product of power structure studies) involves the range of types of power structures that exist at the local level. It seems likely that there is no single power structure in American society. After thoughtful review of the major community studies, Mann concludes that the most reasonable hypothesis is that there exists a continuum of power structure types and that Hunter's findings would be at one end and Dahl's at the other.[23] At both extremes the number of influential people relative to the population is very small.

A second important question about power structure is: what is the relative importance of the governmental and the non-governmental actors in community decision-making? Here again a lack of comparative analysis precludes a definitive answer. A number of the studies of single communities suggest several possible relationships. If a community has a highly monolithic power structure, it is quite possible that the highest elected officials would be a part of that structure. Elected officials could also be important figures in a polylithic system. The elected official automatically possesses important political resources including the formal powers of his office, the backing of the electorate, and the prestige connected with his office. Thus the political resources connected with high public office enhance the governmental official's influence in the process of public policy formulation.

Non-governmental actors can influence public policy indirectly by using their political resources effectively on issues in which they have important stakes. This relationship between the public and private actors is essentially what Dahl found in New Haven. It is also possible, however, that such indirect and selective influence can be employed by a more closely knit "power elite." In one mid-western city, for example, the administration was heavily dependent upon financial leaders to keep the city going. Municipal finances were in such a state that the city had to borrow heavily to meet its current obligations. If the bankers refused to loan the city the necessary funds, financial bankruptcy would result. Thus the bankers had a formidable political resource—money. The mayor, however, was very powerful in his own right and there was no evidence that anyone other than himself was "calling the shots." There was evidence, however, that the mayor looked after the interests of the bankers. Thus indirectly the bankers

---

[23]Lawrence D. Mann, "Studies in Community Decision Making," *Journal of the American Institute of Planners* (February, 1964), pp. 58-65.

influenced public policy. They did not tell the mayor what to do, but the mayor was careful to make decisions which would not adversely affect their interests.

A third type of relationship between governmental and non-governmental actors is where private interests make public policy to serve their ends and use the public officials to make this policy legal. Hunter's findings in Atlanta indicated that non-governmental actors were exercising this type of influence. The idea that a local government is "in someone's pocket" and that the real decisions are dictated by the "big guy" in a smoke filled room is a part of many people's image of government. Actual proven cases of this pattern of power are rare. But it is possible that some municipalities are run by a "power elite." For this reason the strong, private, elite decision-makers should be included in the list of alternative relationships between the governmental and non-governmental actors in local politics.

The above discussion of power structures has suggested the likelihood that there are a range of different power structures from the monolithic to the pluralistic. We have also indicated that the control of governmental decisions by non-governmental groups and individuals can vary from direct and absolute control to the situation where the elected officials have a maximum of latitude in formulating public policy. The important question for our purposes is the relevance of these general observations to the formulation of planning policy. There are four areas in which power structure might influence planning decisions. First, the distribution and use of political power can directly influence planning policy. Secondly, power structure can influence citizen participation in planning. Third, the wielders of power can make developmental decisions through the private market. Although such decisions are outside of the planners' sphere of influence, they affect public planning policy nevertheless. Finally, decisions being made at any time are partly determined by past decisions. Thus an earlier distribution of power may be highly significant in determining the kind of planning policy which can be made currently. Each of the four relationships between power structure and planning policy is discussed below.

The direct influence of power structure on planning decisions is the most obvious type of relationship between the distribution of political resources and planning policy formulation. One example of this relationship is the theory behind the citizen planning commission. As noted in Chapter 3, the idea of having the planner responsible to a citizen commission, was originally based on the assumption that every community has a group of generally "respected and influential" citizens. These citizens should be able to sell the planners' proposals to the politicians better than the planner himself. Thus the citizen commission was established under the assumption that power structures are monolithic. It is logical, that if a small group is really making all important public decisions in a community, the planner will be highly successful if he can get the sympathy and support of that group. When a citizen planning commission is working in practice as it should in theory, planning policy is being directly influenced by the distribution of political power.

The general topic of "citizen participation" in planning provides another link between power structure and planning policy. It is important to note that citizen participation is considered highly important by most professional planners. The ideological importance of a citizen role in planning has been institutionalized by making citizen participation a part of the workable program which is required by the Federal government as a prerequisite for urban renewal funds. Traditionally, citizen participation has meant that the planners would get "interested and informed" groups of citizens together and explain to them what planning involves. The planners tend to view these sessions primarily as a means of educating the public on the benefits of planning generally, and of the plan which has been prepared, specifically. Citizens, however, have rarely participated directly in the making of plans. The participation has come after the plans were well underway. Even such *post facto* participation has usually been limited to an extremely small segment of the community. Planners have not been able to maintain the interest of the public at large over any extended period of time. Thus citizen participation has traditionally occurred after the fact and has involved only a few "key" members of the community.

Some changes in the present pattern of citizen participation may be under way. The spectacles of urban renewal and highway development with their massive uprooting of entire neighborhoods have led in some places to a new kind of citizen participation in planning. Across the nation, neighborhood groups have formed and are still forming to resist planning policy that will level their homes. As Wilson has observed, many people are beginning to resent being classified as slum dwellers to be moved about at the will of city planners and other local governmental officials.[24] Wilson describes these feelings as hidden political costs of the first renewal projects. At this point, he

---

[24]James Q. Wilson, "Planning and Politics: Citizen Participation in Urban Renewal," *Journal of the American Institute of Planners* (November, 1963), pp. 242-249.

argues, there is a growing resistance to renewal largely from residents of neighborhoods slated for demolition. Some recent case studies have demonstrated that neighborhood groups can be devastatingly effective.[25] Groups resisting urban renewal often tend to be formed for that specific purpose and dissolve when the urban renewal issue is resolved. Other local neighborhood groups have recently been formed for broader purposes. Under the stimulus of the poverty program, groups living in the "slum" areas of the cities have been organized for the general purpose of establishing a "low-income lobby" which makes many different demands on city hall. It is not known at this point how effective these groups have been or will be. They have taken an interest in the plans which the city has for their neighborhood and they evaluate these plans from a highly individual perspective.

Another citizen group which may directly influence planning is made up of people who are ideologically committed to planning. Examples of such groups are the civic associations and booster clubs. Members of these organizations will tend to support plans and programs which aim to improve the city as a whole. Other municipal-wide groups strictly represent economic interests; for example, chambers of commerce, businessmen's associations, and real estate organizations. They look at planning proposals in light of the economic interests which they represent.

These various citizen organizations do not always agree with one another on planning proposals because they have different stakes in the outcome. If citizens are really to participate in planning, conflict among groups raises the question of how citizens can be effectively utilized in the planning process. Perception of issues and problems, objectives, knowledge and experience differ from group to group. Some recent studies of low-income neighborhoods in East St. Louis, Illinois, have pointed up wide disparities in perceptions of neighborhood problems among the residents, the city administration, a businessmen's association, and a group of outside professional planners.[26]

Thus citizen participation involves competition among different citizen elements. Each of these elements is attempting to get its particular values reflected in the plan. The complex web of established and *ad hoc* citizen groups will often be a vital part of the community's

[25] J. Clarence Davies III, *Neighborhood Groups and Urban Renewal* (New York: Columbia University Press, 1966).

[26] Robert Mendelson and David C. Ranney, *Central City: A Neighborhood Analysis* (Edwardsville, Illinois: Public Administration and Metropolitan Affairs Program, Southern Illinois University, 1967); and Mendelson and Ranney, *et al.*, *Rush City* (Edwardsville, Illinois: Public Administration and Metropolitan Affairs Program, Southern Illinois University, 1967).

power structure. The nature of citizen involvement in the planning process can directly influence planning policy decisions. Where power is highly centralized, small specialized citizen groups will be least effective. Groups will have difficulty in forming and in making their demands effectively if these demands contradict the interests of members of the established center of power. Under more polylithic political systems, citizen groups will have a greater chance of success since there will be more opportunity to find others who will be willing to use their resources for a common end.

The discussion thus far of the pertinence of power structure to planning has been mainly concerned with the outcome of immediate conflict situations. If we examine long-range development decisions, there are some additional considerations. One of these is what Wingfield has called "inadvertent planning."[27] This paradoxical term refers to the fact that many, if not most, of the decisions which shape community development are made outside of the public planning process. Wingfield suggests four groups which, in one way or another are making decisions which have a significant impact on urban development. These include public decision-makers, private firms, developmental intermediaries (such as bankers, lawyers, and real estate brokers) and the private citizen. Location and expansion decisions of private firms have a substantial impact on the character of a community. Intermediaries such as engineers, lawyers, real estate brokers and various consultants are the technicians who actually advise and help implement the decisions made by the private firms. Private citizens continuously make decisions about where they will live and shop or how they will move about the city which also, when taken as a whole, have a considerable impact on local development patterns. Wingfield argues that the planner's influence over developmental policy is partly a function of the role he plays in these "inadvertent planning" decisions. Through exercising an educational role, the planner can enhance his own power by helping to guide such decisions. Furthermore, the actions of private firms, intermediaries and individual citizens impose a considerable constraint on the developmental decisions which can be made through public policy. This fact decreases the importance (in the long run) which we can attach to a community power structure which exists at any time. Significant limits are set by the "inadvertent planners" on what the public planner and the power structure can do.

---

[27]Clyde J. Wingfield, "Power Structure and Decision Making in City Planning," in Claude E. Hawley and Ruth G. Weintraub, *Administrative Questions and Political Answers* (New York: D. Van Nostrand Co., Inc., 1966), pp. 226-232.

A second consideration in our evaluation of the importance of power structure to long-run planning policy has been suggested by Lawrence Mann.[28] Mann argues that the importance of the concept of power structure to planning can be overstressed. Discussions of power structure usually leave out the time dimension of community decision-making. Yet the development of communities takes place as a result of a whole series of interrelated decisions which are made over a considerable time span. Given the time perspective, influence over the outcome of decisions at a point in time is only a part of the total process of planning policy formulation. In the long run, therefore, the distribution of political resources at any given time may not be a very important element in determining planning policy. Both the points made by Wingfield and Mann would suggest that the importance of power structure as a determinant of planning policy can be greatly overstressed. This is particularly true when we analyze planning policy development over a period of time. On the other hand, the distribution and use of political resources in a community can be a key element in determining how the political system will react to specific proposals made by the planner.

Community Socio-economic Characteristics

The nature of the social and economic characteristics of a community is a further determinant of political involvement in planning. This idea has already been partially discussed in Chapters 5 and 6 where we demonstrated that different kinds of municipalities in metropolitan areas are faced with different planning issues. To a great extent, these issues define the task of the planner. His conscious and unconscious goals address themselves to the problems and planning issues confronting the community. In addition, since these problems and issues confronting the planner are strongly influenced by community characteristics, they also influence the actors, stakes, resources and strategies that are involved in the planning process.

Social and economic characteristics influence political involvement in planning in other ways. The relationship between these characteristics and planning issues means that the content of the plan, as well as the day-to-day implementation activities of the planner will also, in part, be influenced by the social and economic characteristics of the community. Furthermore, as suggested earlier in this chapter, that

[28]Lawrence D. Mann, *op. cit.*

aspect of local political culture that is concerned with planning may be linked with the social and economic characteristics of the people who reside in a given locality. Thus, for all of these reasons, community socio-economic characteristics are important determinants of the nature of political involvement in planning.

Conclusion

The level of political involvement in the planning process varies considerably from issue to issue and community to community. On the basis of numerous case studies, personal observation, and reasoning, hypotheses have been developed to explain this variation. Additional research is needed to test these hypotheses further and to develop them in greater detail. Generally, however, political involvement in planning varies due to differences in the dimensions of planning policy, the role played by the planner, the structure of power in the community and the socio-economic character of the community. These generalizations can provide a deeper understanding of the politics of planning.

8 Some Concluding Remarks

In the course of this text we have analyzed the basic elements of planning policy formulation as it occurs in metropolitan areas. In order to enhance our understanding of planning policy formulation, a model of this process was devised and presented in Chapter 1. Various aspects of the model became the basis for Chapters 2-7. For analytical purposes we separated the basis for the planner's service oriented decisions from the process of bargaining and compromise which we called the politics of planning. It should be stressed that these two elements of planning decision-making are actually occurring simultaneously. Planners do not consciously make a set of decisions which they label "service" and then change them as they take political considerations into account. Any planning policy is a combination of service and political rationale.

Nevertheless it is possible to gain a deeper understanding of planning policy formulation if the service and political aspects of decision-making are kept conceptually separate. In the service category, we have seen that the planner's heritage has had an important influence on him. The strong physical bias, the tradition of utilizing utopian solutions to urban problems, and an aversion to politics are major elements of the planner's heritage. This heritage has affected the planner's training and his professional ideologies. The planning standards, have been greatly influenced by the early development of the profession. In addition, the manner in which the planner interprets and perceives events which occur in the course of his practice is also affected by his professional heritage.

The governmental context of planning is a second important part of the service aspect of planning policy formulation. The formal position of the planning agency in the local public bureaucracy is one facet of planning's governmental context. It is not clear how one form of agency organization versus another actually influences the effectiveness of planning. It seems likely that no single form of agency structure works best under all circumstances. The structure in operation in a given community, however, does determine the formal lines of communication between the planner and the rest of the government. Thus the influence of the formal organization of the planning agency should be analyzed, but on an individual community basis.

Intergovernmental relations is another important aspect of the governmental context of planning. State-local relations determine the basic legal framework under which the planner operates. The organization of the planning agency is largely controlled by state statutes. Federal-local relations are even more important to local planning efforts than state-local relations. Federal programs in urban areas provide a major portion of the money needed to make plans and to implement them. Thus the recent tendency of Federal programs to require more comprehensive planning at the local level and to encourage planning on an area-wide basis are apt to have a profound influence on local planning policy.

The influence of metropolitanism on the formulation of planning policy has been a central concern of this book. Metropolitan areas include many adjacent and overlapping governmental jurisdictions which are politically independent but which are interdependent in practically every other way. The distribution of the population and economic activity among these multiple governmental jurisdictions generates different kinds of planning issues in different parts of the metropolis. Furthermore, the functional interdependence of the politically independent municipalities has produced both a need for metropolitan-wide planning and strong political resistance to the implementation of meaningful metropolitan planning policy.

Thus the planner's heritage, the organization of the local planning agency, intergovernmental relations, and metropolitanism are major influences on the service aspects of planning policy decisions. The politics of planning in metropolitan areas are shaped by metropolitanism and a number of other variables. The stakes which groups and individuals have in a given planning policy determine which actors will become politically involved. The political resources possessed by these actors and the skill with which they use their resources influences how conflict over planning policy is resolved. Those elected officials who ultimately decide the direction of planning policy and the planner himself must bargain and compromise with the participants in the politics of planning. Thus planning policy is partially a product of bargaining and compromise. Furthermore, a number of additional factors must be considered if we are to understand why the political aspects of planning policy formulation are quite different in different communities and why the nature of the politics of planning varies from issue to issue within a specific community. Although comparative research which might provide a sound understanding of these variations is lacking, some hypotheses have been presented in Chapter 7. The development of these hypotheses has indicated that the dimensions of planning policy, local political culture, the role played by the planner, community power structures, and community socio-economic characteristics are the major factors which explain variations in political involvement in the planning process.

Planning in Evolution: Theoretical Issues

While the emphasis of this text has been on understanding how planning policy in metropolitan areas is presently being formulated, it is important to note that planning is undergoing some changes. The environment for which the planner of today must plan has changed considerably since the early 1900's when American planning was beginning. The pioneers of the planning profession were motivated primarily by the physical problems of the early 20th century city. Planners today must also cope with the planning issues which have been generated by metropolitanism. They must meet these issues in a context of rapid social change in which low-income groups and minority groups are demanding that their priorities and values be given the same weight as those of all other elements of society. The planners of today also face a more complex environment where the policies of one municipality affect other municipalities and where land use planning has an immediate and profound affect on the whole socio-economic fabric of large regions of this country. These changes have generated some rethinking of the entire planning process, thus raising a number of theoretical issues which, when resolved, may change the nature of the planning process considerably.

The appropriate scope of the subject matter of planning is a major issue. We have said that planning today focuses on the use of physical space. In Chapter 1, however, we noted that some planners have recommended a broadening of this traditional focus. These planners have recommended giving social, economic, and fiscal planning an emphasis which is equal to physical planning. The problems of the poor in the central cities, declining businesses, and the fiscal crises which many municipalities are facing are strong indications that someone in the local government should be forming policy dealing directly with these problems. The kinds of research and future oriented thinking which the planner has traditionally done would put him in a good position to help formulate such policy. Furthermore, the land use policies which are in the planner's domain are highly interrelated with the broader socio-economic problems which face local governments. If the scope of the planning function is to be broadened, however, more specific definitions of social, economic, and fiscal planning will be needed. The training of the planner will have to be broadened and the profession will have to look far beyond its heritage for new ideologies and professional standards. More specialists in the various types of planning will be needed and teams of these specialists will have to be employed to approach planning issues from a broader perspective.

The effort of planners to decide upon the most appropriate geographical scope for the planning function provides another important theoretical issue. Most planners would agree that the nature of metropolitan areas demands metropolitan-wide planning. But there are a host of questions about metropolitan-wide planning on which there is little if any agreement. Should the entire planning function be raised to the metropolitan level? If so how can this be accomplished politically? If not, what kinds of planning should the metropolitan agency do and what kinds should the local agencies do? What agency should engage in zoning, housing policy, or human resource development? What kinds of governmental institutions are needed to handle a metropolitan planning agency? What are the political implications of any given distribution of functions between a metropolitan and a local planning agency? These are just some of the more crucial questions which must be faced in deciding on the appropriate geographical scope for the planning function.

Another current theoretical issue centers on the role of the citizen in the planning process. The previous chapter noted that planners have traditionally paid great lip service to the notion that the citizen should be involved in the planning process. In practice, however, this involvement has usually been limited to an invitation for citizens to attend public hearings and meetings after the plan has been developed. Recently there has been some discussion of the possibility of encouraging more substantive citizen involvement in the planning process. Paul Davidoff, for example, has proposed the development of a system of "advocacy planning" where different planners work directly with groups holding differing objectives and produce planning policy alternatives which reflect a variety of value systems. Some planners would serve as free consultants to neighborhood groups and act as advocates of their group's objectives. The Model Cities Program encourages this sort of citizen participation. Once again, however, there are many unanswered questions. Assuming that the more substantive type of citizen participation is desirable, how do we operationalize it? With what planning questions should an advocate planner deal? How should his activity relate to the work of the municipal planner and the metropolitan planner? What criteria should be used to weigh planning alternatives which come out of an "advocacy planning" system? What institutions would be needed? What does an advocate planner do about major disagreement over objectives within the group (such as black power versus integration)? How does the advocate planner go about finding out what his group wants him to advocate? Thus, while the issue of citizen participation is important and needs rethinking, it is also very complicated.

One further theoretical issue involves the role of the planner in the politics of planning. In Chapters 6 and 7 we noted that the planner has a choice of being a political agnostic, a political confidant to decision-makers or a political activist. At present there is no normative theory which can provide guidelines for the planner who wishes to know what role he ought to assume. If the scope of planning both in terms of subject matter and geography is broadened and if communities adopt more substantive systems of citizen participation, planning policy formulation will involve an increasing amount of political involvement and conflict. Yet the whole issue of rational planning policy in a political context has barely begun to be explored. If planning is to effectively deal with the complex issues which are facing metropolitan areas, the planners' role in the political system will have to be carefully thought through.

Planning in Evolution: Technical Issues

The theoretical issues discussed above do not exhaust the list of questions which the increasing complexities of urban life raise for the local planner. They are, however, among the most important. These issues are concerned with what planners should do, when they should do it and why they should do it. There is another set of issues, however, that involves how the planner should go about doing the research he needs to do, making the plans and implementing these plans once they become policy. The greater complexities of the urban environment created by metropolitanism have generated new techniques and have also pointed up many deficiencies in the planner's present bag of tools. A complete inventory of emerging techniques and technical deficiencies would be unmanageable in this volume; however, some of the more important techniques and deficiencies are briefly outlined below.

The recognition that the urban environment contains many different, highly interrelated elements has brought a search for analytical techniques which will show how policies involving one of these elements will affect the others. Terms such as systems analysis, planning-programming-budgeting systems (PPBS), cost effectiveness, benefit-cost analysis, and program evaluation and review technique (PERT), are beginning to appear in planning literature. These are the names of analytical techniques which attempt to deal with interdependencies among policy areas in a systematic fashion. The United States Department of Defense has been using these techniques for military planning for a number of years but their application to the planning of metropolitan areas is in an infant stage. The Model Cities Program requires the use of some of these techniques. Such systematic approaches to planning involve the establishment of concrete objectives and a careful weighing of all of the advantages and disadvantages of various alternative programs and policies. Then priorities are established among programs and a schedule for their implementation is devised. The system of programs and policies which is in effect is constantly under review in order to determine the current validity of past calculations of advantages and disadvantages.

Another technical issue focuses on land use standards. At present, standards for location and the amount of space required for particular uses are quite crude. Numerous rules of thumb of obscure origin are currently in use. Low densities for residential areas, a given amount of recreational area for every local resident, and a variety of notions about land use incompatibilities are examples of such rules. Much work remains to be done in the development of more meaningful standards. The creation of mathematical models of land use development is a step in this direction. These models utilize the computer's ability to make a great number of mathematical calculations very rapidly. They search for stable relationships between specific variables such as the location of a highway and residential development patterns. The model builder will look for those relationships which are of interest to him and try to describe them in concrete terms. Models can simply describe the relationships between developmental variables, and can attempt to specify causation so the planner can predict the consequences of a given planning policy. The development models can potentially aid our understanding of land use relationships and provide a stronger factual basis for land use standards. Much more work is needed in model building, however, to provide this information.

Various forms of economic analysis are evolving which can be useful in the development of these standards. Economic base studies determine the strengths and weaknesses of a community's mixture of economic activities. Such studies can predict the impact of a change in the mixture on employment and income. Other studies record the impact of alternative industrial locations in terms of the cost of producing goods. Economic linkages between industries can be determined with the use of such techniques as input-output analysis and industrial complex analysis. All of these methods of economic analysis need further development, and must be linked to land use standards so that they may become an integral part of the planning process.

One further area which needs a great deal of attention is the social and psychological impact of planning policy. If planning is to benefit the individual, research methods are needed to determine how particular policies are apt to affect this individual. Highways and urban renewal projects have shattered neighborhoods and generated violence, depression, alienation and other socio-psychological side effects. The extent of these undesirable consequences of past planning policies is not known. But enough information is available to indicate the importance of developing the ability to foresee socio-psychological consequences of planning policy. With this foresight, these consequences can become important considerations in the process of formulating planning policy.

Mechanisms for the Evolution of Planning

The evolution of theoretical and technical issues described above is not a chance event. New thinking about the what, when, why and how of planning is the result of a complex of different forces. In general, the evolution of planning is occurring as a result of feedback from the planning or non-planning of the past. Because present planning approaches and techniques are not meeting the problems of cities, new approaches and techniques are being sought. The greater complexity of the urban environment resulting from metropolitanism has been an important stimulus to the present evolution of planning theory and techniques. Slums, congestion, urban violence, fiscal problems, declining business, local unemployment and other difficulties all represent the failure of past planning efforts to meet the needs of the developing metropolis. These problems have a feedback effect which causes planners and students of planning to take measures which might eliminate future failures. Thus planning policy formulation is a dynamic process where the policies made today have a profound influence on the policies of tomorrow.

Index

Index